RIP-ROARING
RACES AND RALLIES

RIP-ROARING RACES AND RALLIES

BY
ELWOOD D. BAUMANN

Franklin Watts
New York/London/Toronto/1981

Photographs courtesy of:

National Automotive History Collection, Detroit
Public Library: pp. 6–7, 34–35, 102–103;

National Motor Museum, Beaulieu, Hampshire, England:
pp. 10–11, 16–17, 26–27, 72–73, 78–79;

Indianapolis Motor Speedway: pp. 48–49, 52–53;

Goodyear Tire and Rubber Co.: pp. 106–107;

Long Photography: pp. 110–111

Library of Congress Cataloging in Publication Data

Baumann, Elwood D.
Rip-roaring races and rallies.

Bibliography: p.
Includes index.
Summary: Discusses the history of automobile races
and rallies beginning with the
first organized car contest held in France in 1894.
1. Automobile racing—History—Juvenile literature.
2. Automobile rallies—History—Juvenile literature.
[1. Automobile racing—History.
2. Automobile rallies—History] I. Title.
GV1029.15.B38   796.7'2   81–7581
ISBN 0–531–04344–4   AACR2

CONTENTS

To Trevor and Annette Cooper,
who were always happy to help
when I needed something
from the English end for
RIP-ROARING RACES AND RALLIES.

RIP-ROARING
RACES AND RALLIES

(1)
THE FIRST "REAL" RACES

When the man who owned the first car in the world met the man who owned the second car in the world, he probably challenged him to a race. We don't actually know that this happened, of course, but it very well could have.

Car racing became a popular sport at a time when there were only a few thousand cars in the entire world. Speed has always fascinated people and they gasped in delight when they saw the first cars whizzing along at speeds of 5 miles (8 km) an hour and even more. This was heady stuff and they loved it.

The first organized car contest could have been called either a race or a rally. This was true in the nineteenth century and it's true today. The words race and rally are used interchangeably. Britain's World Cup Rally is a race and the driver who crosses the finish line first is the winner. "It doesn't make any difference whether you call it a race or a rally," says Erwin Lessner, author of *Famous Auto Races and Rallies.* "Winning it is the only thing that matters."

It was a French newspaper that sponsored Europe's first car race—or rally. Prizes were to be given on the basis of dependability, safety, and cost of operation. The cars were to travel from Paris to Rouen, a distance of nearly 79 miles (127 km). To the organizers' utter amazement, 102 contestants signed up for the event. The year was 1894, but cars were already a fairly common sight in the French capital.

Only nineteen vehicles remained after the trial runs. The other eighty-three had been disqualified for one reason or another. One of the vehicles still in the running was a nine-passenger steam bus. Every seat was occupied and everyone seemed to be having a marvelous time.

There was a bit of drama before the event actually got underway. A driver by the name of Etienne Le Blant drove up to the starting line and straight into a car driven by his brother Maurice.

Poor Etienne! His troubles were just beginning. Eighteen of the vehicles set off for Rouen right on schedule, but his steam car stubbornly refused to start. Etienne's face was a bright red and he kept talking to himself under his breath. The crowd jeered and cheered and the racer's face got redder and redder. The steamer finally came to life. Etienne quickly jumped in and went steaming off after the others.

He was in trouble again almost at once. While turning off the Boulevard Maillot, he misjudged somehow and plowed into a sidewalk cafe. Fortunately, no one was hurt and Etienne was soon back in the running.

But he wasn't there for long. He had been on the road to Rouen for only a few minutes when disaster struck. Etienne lost control of his car while moving at a good clip and jumped a ditch. The front axle was broken and the unlucky driver was out of the rally. Etienne left his stricken steamer sitting in a potato field and stamped sadly back to Paris.

Most of the other drivers had much better luck. Fifteen of the nineteen starters reached Rouen and they were given a tremendous welcome. Young girls threw them bouquets of flowers and there was food and wine galore. The men had made it all the way from Paris at high speeds and everyone looked upon them as heroes.

The man who made the best time on the trip was Count Albert de Dion. He had covered the entire distance at an average speed of $11\frac{1}{2}$ miles (18.5 km) an hour. This was far faster than anyone would have thought possible. The judges, however, decided against giving him first prize. His car was not really a car, they said. It was actually a steam tractor pulling a passenger coach.

When the Winner Loses—
and Still Wins

The Paris to Rouen rally of 1894 had been a howling success. There could be absolutely no doubt about that. It was only natural, therefore, that another motoring event should be planned for 1895. This was to be a true test of men and machines. It was going to be a race in every sense of the word. Drivers would race from Paris to Bordeaux and back to Paris. The first man to finish would be the winner.

Sad to say, things didn't turn out quite that way. Emile Levassor was the first man across the finish line, but he didn't win a thing. He had driven his four-horsepower Panhard almost nonstop for forty-eight hours and forty-five minutes. He had done this all on his own because he would not even let his relief driver get into the car with him. Levassor may have thought that no one else on earth could drive at an average speed of 15 miles (24 km) an hour.

Levassor probably wasn't too upset by the fact that he wasn't given a single cent of the prize money. The race rules stated clearly that only vehicles with four seats were eligible. His two-seater didn't qualify, but Levassor didn't care. He had designed and built his four-horsepower Panhard and now he had proved that his car was the fastest and toughest vehicle in the world. This was excellent publicity and worth more to him than being declared the official winner. He knew that everyone interested in car racing would know who had crossed the finish line first.

The officials awarded first prize to the driver of a Peugeot who arrived back in Paris six hours after Emile Levassor. Second prize was won by a Peugeot which reached Paris eleven hours after the Panhard.

Peugeots, it's interesting to note, are still extremely popular cars in France today and win international races and rallies every year.

The Winner Takes All

The French adore speed and huge crowds thronged the Avenue de Paris to see the start of the Paris-Marseilles-Paris Race in 1896. The event covered 1,080 miles (1,739 km) and twenty-eight vehicles were ready to roll. Twenty-four of the vehicles had four wheels each and four of them were three-wheelers which the French insisted upon calling tricycles. The two favorites were Emile Levassor in his Panhard and Count Albert de Dion in his steam tractor.

It was a beautiful day when the contestants rolled out of Paris, but a fearful storm struck that night. Rain pelted down relentlessly. The open vehicles offered no protection from the elements and everyone was soon soaked and miserable. A screaming wind tore up trees by their roots and made conditions even more hazardous.

Visibility was virtually nonexistent, yet many drivers soldiered on. One who did so to his great sorrow was Leon Bollée. He had a 25-mile (40-km) lead when the storm struck and he wasn't going to let anything stop him. But something did! Bollée smashed into a tree in the almost total darkness. The driver and his three passengers were hurled through the air, but nobody was hurt. The car, however, was smashed to pieces.

The driving rain caused numerous mechanical difficulties. In one case, the motor sputtered and died when a car was halfway up a hill. The four occupants immediately jumped out and began pushing. They pushed with such enthusiasm that they pushed the car right over the crest. It went zooming down the hill entirely on its own while the four men stood helplessly on the hilltop. They heard a distinct crash a moment later and they guessed correctly that their car had been stopped by a tree.

In spite of all the rain, wind, and mud, nine vehicles finished the race. This time, however, the first driver to cross the finish line was declared the winner. He had astounded the motoring world by covering 1,080 miles (1,739 km) at an average speed of almost exactly 16 miles (26 km) an hour.

Not Everyone
Loved Racing

Car racing got off to a very slow start in the United States. The first race was run in Chicago in 1895. This was the year in which the French had raced from Paris to Bordeaux and back. By comparison, the American event was a very tame affair. Although it was sponsored by the Chicago *Times-Herald* newspaper and received a lot of publicity, very few people seemed to be interested. The day of America's great love affair with cars and car races had not yet dawned.

In England, at that time the world's most highly industrialized nation, the car-racing picture was even bleaker. An Act of Parliament passed in 1865 imposed speed limits of 2 miles (3 km) an hour in the towns and 4 miles (6 km) an hour in the country. Every car had to be preceded by a man carrying a red flag. This law was modified somewhat in 1878. It then stated that the flag carried by the man walking in front of the car no longer had to be red. It could be black, green, orange, sky-blue pink, or any other hue.

The British magazine *Autocar* called November 16, 1896 Emancipation Day. On that momentous occasion, the speed limit in Britain was raised to 14 miles (22 km) an hour. The Motor Car Club celebrated by organizing a race from London to Brighton, but it was somewhat of a flop. The great majority of people looked upon car racing as a boring sport which would never catch on.

Over: *the first "official" car race in the United States, held in 1895, was sponsored by the Chicago* Times-Herald. *Sadly, it aroused almost no interest.*

(2)
AN AMERICAN IN PARIS

James Gordon Bennett, owner of the New York *Herald,* was a master at increasing the circulation of his newspaper. One of his most famous stunts was to send Henry Stanley into the wilds of darkest Africa to find Dr. David Livingstone. Livingstone wasn't even lost, but the *Herald*'s readers didn't know that, of course. They dutifully bought their newspapers every day and they all breathed a great sigh of relief when the *Herald* solemnly informed them that the missing doctor had at last been found.

Bennett moved to Paris in 1887 and set up a European edition of the *Herald.* He was constantly on the lookout for exciting news and he sent a reporter on a bicycle to cover the Paris to Rouen car race. The following year, he helped to sponsor the race from Paris to Bordeaux and back. Interest in the event ran so high that Bennett decided to sponsor his own races in the future.

This was rather a curious decision, but Bennett did many curious things. Although he often said that cars were here to stay, he didn't like them at all. They were noisy and dirty, he said, and their use should be restricted to certain areas. Bennett himself avoided cars like the plague. He never learned how to drive one and he never saw a race in his life.

Another most peculiar thing was Bennett's attitude toward the races which were named after him. He had had a beautiful trophy designed for the winner. It was made of marble, gold, and silver and was worth a great deal of money. Naturally enough, the annual racing events became known to the world as the Gordon Bennett Trophy Races.

This wasn't true in every case, however. Bennett instructed his editors to call the race the *"Coupe Internationale"* and nothing else. Bennett personally always referred to the trophy as the Columbia Cup, but he never told anyone why. We can be sure, though, that it wasn't modesty that prompted Bennett to use his own terms. He loved the limelight and he was certainly far from a modest man.

The Gordon Bennett Trophy Races

The first Gordon Bennett Trophy Race was run in France on June 14, 1900. It was a disaster. In spite of all the publicity given to it by the *Herald,* the crowd was disappointingly small.

Only five drivers showed up for the event and only two of them were foreigners. One was a Belgian known as Red Devil Jenatzy because of his flaming red beard, his shock of red hair, and his daredevil attitude. The other foreigner was an American by the name of Alexander Winton. Winton had entered the race in a car which he had built himself. He didn't call it a car, though. He always referred to it as a steam wagon.

The race started at three o'clock in the morning. Red Devil Jenatzy was the first one away and he waved a cheery good-bye to the small crowd of spectators. But poor Red Devil wasn't cheerful for long. He missed a turn shortly after setting off and was soon hopelessly lost in the sidestreets of Paris. Someone eventually steered him toward the road to Lyons, but his car broke down before he got there.

*Over: a French-made Darracq
arrives in the Austrian capital
after completing the Paris
to Vienna Race of 1902.*

Alexander Winton didn't fare much better. His steam wagon started making horrible clanking noises while it was still within sight of the French capital. He was staring sadly at his stricken vehicle when a car stopped alongside and the driver offered him a lift to Lyons. The name of the driver was Fernand Charron and he was also in the Gordon Bennett Trophy Race. Winton may not have done too well in his steam wagon, but at least he was in the car that got to Lyons first.

The second Gordon Bennett Trophy Race was even more of a disaster than the first. There were only two entries and both of them were French. The *Herald* tried to make a big thing out of its *"Coupe Internationale,"* but the event was largely ignored by the public.

Bennett Battles On

Readers of the *Herald* received almost daily doses of articles on motoring. Bennett may have been an eccentric, but he was also a practical man. He knew that cars would become increasingly important. As a newspaperman, he felt that it was his duty to keep his readers aware of what was going on in the infant automobile industry.

Bennett was very unhappy over the fact that the Europeans were far more interested in cars than the Americans were. In most cases, an American who owned a car had built it himself. The "factory" was usually a barn or a warehouse. A car was still regarded pretty much as a toy that very few people could afford.

By 1900, Germany, Italy, and Britain had a number of cars on the road, but France was way in the lead. A reporter told Bennett that he had counted twenty-three cars in just one hour in downtown Paris. This bit of information staggered Bennett. He doubted very much that a person could see that many cars in New York City in an entire day.

Bennett was determined to make people look upon the car as something typically American. If an American driving an American-built car could win an international race, Bennett reasoned, interest in cars and racing in the United States would increase dramatically. With that thought in mind, Bennett began making plans for the 1902 event. He was sure that it would be the greatest race ever run.

Although the event was not won by an American, the Gordon Bennett Trophy Race of 1902 was a roaring success. There were 130 entries and they were driving everything from motorcycles to tricycles to huge racing cars. The route was to be from Paris to Innsbruck, Austria. Members of the Automobile Club of France, however, could continue on to Vienna if they wished. That meant a lot of mountain driving. There would be no racing through the Swiss Alps, however. Drivers were told that anyone who exceeded the speed limit in Switzerland could find himself in very serious trouble.

Although the race started at the unearthly hour of three in the morning, a huge crowd was on hand to see it off. This time the race was truly international in scope and that appealed to the public. The race ran through three different countries and drivers from seven different countries were represented. The varied assortment of vehicles was also of great interest.

The race was won by Selwyn Edge, a man who came from a country where the speed limit was still 14 miles (22 km) an hour. For the first Englishman who had ever won a major road race, Edge was very modest. He told the press that he had won only because so many of the other drivers had run into bad luck.

This was certainly true. Vehicles then were not as maneuverable as they are now and drivers in the Paris to Innsbruck race had run into just about everything. They had run into each other and they had also run into trees, sheds, stone fences, sheep, cows, and horses. One of the French drivers even managed to run straight into a henhouse which promptly collapsed around his ears.

Maurice Gabriel

Bennett felt that long-distance racing on open highways had become too dangerous and the 1903 event was held on a closed circuit in Ireland. This was excellent news for the spectators. The figure-eight-shaped circuit meant that they would get to see a little bit more of the race. The drivers, too, were mostly in favor of the closed circuit.

One of the new entries in 1903 was a Frenchman named Maurice Gabriel who was driving a huge 90-horsepower Mors. Although he boasted that his car could do 100 miles (160 km) an hour, Gabriel got off to a very slow start. He was supposed to be the third one away, but nothing happened when the official starter swung his checkered flag and yelled, "Go!" Gabriel simply sat hunched expectantly over the steering wheel.

The starter again swung his flag and yelled, "Go!"

Maurice Gabriel didn't move a muscle.

After his third effort had failed, the bewildered starter appealed for help. Fernand Charron came trotting over, said a few words to Gabriel, then turned to the starter. "Monsieur Gabriel doesn't understand English," he explained, "and he didn't know what you said."

"*Allez!*" yelled the official and Maurice Gabriel went rolling off in his big Mors. Less than halfway through the first lap, he misjudged a curve and rolled down an embankment into the Stradbally River.

Larry Mooers and Alexander Winton, the two American entries, also had trouble getting away from the starting line. Mooers stalled his Peerless and the mechanic had to give it a big push before the engine sputtered into life.

Winton's problem wasn't solved that easily. His steam wagon—which everyone except Winton called a Winton—developed carburetor trouble as soon as the starter gave him the signal. It took forty minutes to solve the problem and by that time the steam wagon didn't have a hope of winning.

The winner was Red Devil Jenatzy, who averaged 49 miles (79 km) an hour in a Mercedes he had borrowed from an American friend.

The Gordon Bennett Trophy Races were also run in 1904 and 1905, but the end was in sight. French automobile manufacturers simply did not like the fact that cars made in Germany and Italy were winning some of the races. Neither did they like the fact that the race was sponsored by an American. Somehow, this did not seem right to the French and they declared that their cars would no longer enter the Gordon Bennett Trophy Races.

Gordon Bennett, the eccentric American who had done so much for car racing, quietly withdrew his trophy in 1906. Typically, however, he managed to get in the last word. On the day that the trophy was withdrawn, the *Herald* boldly predicted that the United States would soon be the world's leading car manufacturer.

Over: *Red Devil Jenatzy was probably the world's first racing hero. He is seen here at the wheel of a Mercedes just before the 1905 Gordon Bennett Trophy Race.*

(3)
ENTER THE
WORLD'S RICHEST MAN

William Vanderbilt was the ideal person to promote car racing in the United States. He was an excellent driver himself and had raced both in the United States and Europe. In 1902, he became the first American to hold the world speed record. He was wildly enthusiastic about cars and he wanted the American people to share his enthusiasm. It was that desire that led to the birth of the Vanderbilt Cup Races.

The first race was scheduled to be held on October 8, 1904 on Long Island, New York. The event was given enormous publicity because Vanderbilt owned a governing interest in several newspapers. He wanted the event to be truly international in scope and the leading European racing drivers were invited to the United States with their cars.

Vanderbilt and officials of the American Automobile Association had drawn up all the plans for the race. It was to be run over a roughly triangular course on public roads in the center of Long Island. The course was 28 miles (45 km) long and each driver had to make ten complete circuits. Most of the course was through sparsely populated farmland and Vanderbilt thought that the location was ideal. The fact that he owned most of the land along the way may or may not have influenced his thinking.

When the local farmers read the public notices that had been posted along the race route, they were furious. We can hardly blame them. They were told in blunt terms that they could not use the roads between five in the morning and three in the afternoon. They were also told to keep their fowl, domestic animals, and children off the roads during those hours.

The farmers had a legitimate complaint. They told officials that they had to use the roads to get their produce to market. There was more to it than that, though. There was also the possibility that the fearful noise of the racing cars would frighten their cows so badly that they would not produce milk for a while.

A reporter for *The New York Times* said that some of the farmers were so angry that they threatened to stand in the middle of the road and stop the race with their rifles. Another farmer was somewhat more imaginative. He told the reporter that he was going to stand in the road with his wife and seven children and refuse to move.

Some of the overseas drivers weren't too happy about the race either. They were accustomed to the European way of doing things and they thought that some of the rules of the race were idiotic. It annoyed them that they had to grind to a dead stop at every intersection. They also had to slow down to 10 miles (16 km) an hour at each of the five railroad tracks.

To make matters even worse, the villages of Hempstead and Hicksville had been declared "neutralized control sections." No racing at all was permitted inside the village limits. Men on bicycles would guide the drivers through town and there was no way that they could be hurried.

America's First
Major Road Race

In spite of everything, the first car was flagged off promptly at six in the morning. The second one followed 10 minutes later and then it was Number Three's turn. Number Three was Maurice Gabriel, who had gotten off to such a slow start in the Gordon Bennett Trophy Race the year before. Monsieur Gabriel had picked up a bit of English since then, however, and when the starter yelled, "Go!" Gabriel knew exactly what he meant.

A rather strange event occurred just after Number Nine

had taken off: Number Ten did not seem to be anywhere around. This was a Fiat driven by an Italian named Sartori. The starter looked around nervously and wondered what to do. His nervousness was certainly understandable. The missing car belonged to—of all people—Mr. William K. Vanderbilt.

An hour and forty-five minutes after the start of the first Vanderbilt Cup Race, Sartori drove sadly up to the starting line. He had had engine trouble between Garden City and Westbury, he said, and that was why he was late. Although there was absolutely no chance whatsoever of winning, Vanderbilt told Sartori to get out there and do his stuff. The Italian drove for a lap and a half and then his clutch burned out.

Another strange event occurred very early in the race. A German driver pulled up at one of the official stopping points and a mechanic crawled under the car to make an adjustment. For some unknown reason, the driver suddenly took off and ran over the mechanic. Luckily, the man wasn't hurt badly.

Six hours and fifty-six minutes after the race had begun, the first car was flagged across the finish line. The driver was an American named George Heath who had averaged 52 miles (84 km) an hour. Unfortunately, however, it wasn't a 100 percent American victory. Heath had won the race in a French Panhard.

The results of the first major road race in America pleased Vanderbilt and he immediately began making plans for the next year's event. To his relief, there were no angry threats from the Long Island farmers this time. They recognized a good thing when they saw it and they were all looking forward to the race.

The event meant big money to the enterprising farmers. The race started at six in the morning and many thousands of people came to Long Island the day before. Every barn along the race route became a hotel for the night. Every field became a parking lot. Farmers' wives sold apples, sandwiches, coffee, and everything else to the hungry masses and shamelessly charged horrendous prices. It was reported that even Vanderbilt himself had complained about the cost of a peanut butter and jelly sandwich.

In 1905, the Vanderbilt Cup Race was won by a Frenchman named Victor Hénery driving a French Darracq. He had averaged 61 miles (98 km) an hour for 283 miles (456 km). Second place went to George Heath, who had won the 1904 event. Joe Tracy, an American driving a huge American Locomobile, was third.

American-designed and -built cars were coming into their own at last.

People Problems

It's strange to note that the tremendous popularity of the Vanderbilt Cup Races contributed indirectly to their death. A crowd estimated at three hundred and forty thousand people attended the 1906 contest. No other sporting event had ever attracted such a huge number of people.

The crowd simply could not be restrained. There was just no way that the police could keep a third of a million excited spectators off the road. People did not seem to realize that they were flirting with death. They would stand in the middle of the road watching the cars racing toward them at speeds of up to 80 miles (129 km) an hour, then dash for safety at the last split second. Not surprisingly, there were some who didn't make it.

All of the drivers were very unhappy about the situation. It was terribly disconcerting to come roaring around a corner and find yourself hurtling headlong toward a crowd of people. One driver became so upset that he stopped in front of the racing officials' stand and angrily shouted that there would be a blood bath if the people were not kept off the road.

Vanderbilt was worried. The race was his idea and he felt personally responsible. He couldn't very well call it off, but he had to do something. Getting into his white Mercedes, he drove along the road and pleaded with the people to keep out of the path of the cars.

When Vanderbilt returned to the officials' stand, there was some grim news awaiting him: One of the cars had smashed into a crowd of spectators. Nobody knew how many people had been injured, but the racer had been killed.

The driver of the car was Eliot Shepard, Vanderbilt's cousin.

Police told Vanderbilt that they would not be able to manage the crowds and the race was not run in 1907. It was run again the following year, however, as well as in 1909 and 1910. The event became progressively more popular and the crowds became larger and more unruly. Americans driving American-built cars were now carrying away all the trophies and that brought more and more people out to Long Island.

But not everybody was happy about the Vanderbilt Cup Races. People were appalled by the number of accidents and the growing number of injuries. One newspaper called the races motoring madness and begged its readers to stay away from them.

The voices of opposition became so loud that Vanderbilt decided to take his race elsewhere. It was held in Georgia in 1911, in Wisconsin in 1912, and in California the next three years. The United States entered World War I the following year and the Vanderbilt Cup Races simply faded out of existence.

They had actually become a victim of their own popularity.

(4)
THE PEKING TO PARIS CLASSIC OF 1907

It was difficult to take the article in *Le Matin,* a Paris newspaper, seriously. Surely nobody could race a car from the capital of China to the capital of France. The two cities were thousands of miles apart. All sorts of dangers lay in between. *Le Matin* must be having a private little joke at their readers' expense, people told one another.

But *Le Matin* was not joking. Car racing had a big following in France and the newspaper wanted to give the people a race they would never forget. The race they had in mind would generate a great deal of interest. It would also sell a great number of newspapers. Everyone would want to know what sort of progress the racers were making and there was only one way that they could find out. That, of course, was by buying a copy of *Le Matin.*

After all the publicity seekers and crackpots were weeded out, only five serious entries were left. Three of these were from France, one was from Holland, and the other from Italy. The two German entries were withdrawn before they even left Berlin, but nobody ever found out why.

The competing cars were very interesting to say the least. Two of the French entries were ten-horsepower De Dions which were capable of speeds up to 28 miles (45 km) an hour. The third French entry was a 6-horsepower Contal tricycle which some unkind soul said looked like a camel that had lost a hind leg. Augustin Pons, the proud owner of the tricycle, refused to tell anyone how fast it would go.

Holland entered a fifteen-horsepower Spyker touring car. It was gaily painted in red, white, and black stripes. "Peking to Paris or Bust" was painted on the front, back, and sides in several languages including Chinese and Russian. The Dutch driver and his mechanic cheerfully insisted that their car was the only one capable of making the trip.

Prince Scipione Borghese of Italy said the same thing about his huge 50-horsepower Itala. He would plow his way across Asia, he boasted, then race on to Paris at 50 miles (80 km) an hour. The other cars would still be struggling through Siberia when he pulled up in front of the *Le Matin* Building in the French capital.

The Agonies of Asia

The five cars and their crews arrived in Peking on June 6, 1907. Although the Chinese had never seen a car before, they were not in the least impressed. They were only confused. These strange foreigners had brought their horseless carriages all the way from Paris to Peking on the train. Now they were going to drive them back to where they had come from. It just didn't make any sense at all.

The racers were also confused. Detailed information about road conditions was almost impossible to come by. Decent maps of China, Mongolia, Siberia, and Russia simply didn't exist. About all they knew was that they had to keep heading west for 8,000 or 9,000 miles (12,800 to 14,400 km). This would bring them to Paris eventually and the first one to get there would be the winner of the race.

One of the many problems facing the drivers was supplies. Fuel, oil, tires, and spare parts had been deposited at prearranged spots along the route. This wasn't quite as cozy as it sounds, though. It would be very easy to miss a supply point in the wild wastes of Asia. If that happened, the driver could find himself in big trouble.

In spite of the problems that lay ahead, the men were anxious to be off. The race was scheduled to start at eight-thirty in the morning on June 10, but there was a slight delay. The priest who had been asked to bless the Itala overslept and the prince did not want to leave without his blessing. It was almost noon before the priest finally arrived, so the drivers decided to have lunch before leaving.

The race got off to an impressive start. Special trains had brought Europeans to Peking from Shanghai and other Chinese cities. All the foreign embassies were represented. Everyone was in a festive mood. A French diplomat swung the flag and the five cars started rolling toward Paris. They had to roll very slowly, though, because they were being led by a brass band.

Things didn't speed up very much when the brass band turned off on the outskirts of the city. The road became a disaster almost at once. Chinese officials had told them that a good highway stretched all the way from Peking to Nankow and they hadn't expected anything like this. It gave the drivers a good idea of what lay in front of them, however.

Poor Augustin Pons! He found himself in trouble after covering only 10 miles (16 km) of the route. The steering mechanism of his tricycle went wrong and he couldn't correct it. Pons would aim his strange-looking vehicle in one direction and it would take off in a totally different one. His tricycle acted as though it had a mind of its own.

Finally, Pons had to give up. He told the others that he would have his tricycle repaired in Peking, then ship it to Nankow and rejoin the race there. This would disqualify him, but he was anxious to complete the journey.

There was no need for Pons to hurry. The four other vehicles were moving forward at little more than a snail's pace. As a matter of fact, they weren't even going that fast much of the time. Unbridged rivers and great stretches of deep sand and gooey mud frequently stopped them in their tracks.

Over: *power of all kinds was needed to pull the cars out of the mud of the Hun-Ho River during the Peking to Paris Race of 1907.*

Teams of horses and mules and gangs of Chinese workers pushed, pulled, and dragged the cars across the worst places. This was never easy, but it was an even tougher proposition with the huge Itala. Then Prince Borghese had an idea! He had his mechanic take off the heavy body of the car. The seats were removed as well and the prince and his mechanic had to make themselves as comfortable as possible on a couple of packing cases. The car now weighed considerably less and the workers grinned happily.

A German reporter who rode out from Nankow to interview the drivers sent off a very dreary report of the race. It wasn't really a race at all, he wired Berlin. It was simply a case of seeing which car could be dragged along the fastest. The cars had only covered 150 miles (240 km) in seven days. Almost all of that had been by horsepower and manpower.

Things improved somewhat when the vehicles reached the Mongolian steppes. The land here was as flat as the top of a table. The drivers simply had to follow the line of telegraph poles. The Itala could occasionally do 30 miles (48 km) an hour on such ground and the two De Dions and the Spyker could manage almost 20 miles (32 km) an hour. Pons, who had rejoined the race in Nankow, could barely get up to 10 miles (16 km) an hour on his little tricycle. Even that proved to be too much, however, and the unlucky Pons had to abandon his machine in a Mongolian town with the musical name of Pong-Kiong.

The others pushed on with grim determination. The rock-strewn steppes of Mongolia gave way to the waterless wastes of the Gobi Desert. It was the middle of summer and the brutal heat left the men gasping for breath. Nevertheless, they frequently had to manhandle their cars through sand-traps and salt marshes.

Siberia was not really much better. The sand and salt simply became a sea of black mud in places. Instead of dry river beds, the drivers now faced unbridged rivers. A few of them had been bridged, it's true, but they were only sturdy enough to support the weight of a horse and cart. Prince

Borghese learned that to his sorrow when the heavy Itala broke through the planking of a bridge and crashed down into the river below.

Matters improved just a tiny bit more when the cars reached the Trans-Siberian Railroad. A road had been built parallel to the tracks, but much of it had simply disappeared. In some places, the best progress could be made by bouncing along down the railroad itself.

A Prince and the Police

Forty days after leaving Peking, Prince Borghese left Asia behind him and entered Europe. Although Paris was still almost a continent away, he was certain that the tough part of the journey was over. From here on, it ought to be smooth sailing.

Well, not quite. Less than an hour after entering Europe, the Itala bogged down in a vast morass of sticky black mud. This was some of the richest soil on earth, but that knowledge did absolutely nothing for the Italians' morale. They couldn't have cared less how rich the soil was. All they wanted to do was to get out of it.

There were no Chinese workers to drag the car out of the mud, but help arrived from an unexpected quarter. The two De Dions and the Spyker arrived on the scene during the next three days. The combined efforts of all the men got the cars through the goo and back onto firmer ground.

After that, it was the big Itala all the way. The car rolled along for hundreds of miles over land that was as flat as the American prairie. Prince Borghese insisted upon doing all the driving and was occasionally able to get up to 50 miles (80 km) an hour. The two French teams and the Dutch team fell farther and farther behind.

The Italians crossed into Germany on August 5 and stopped in a town near the border. While the mechanic was checking the car, the prince went for a stroll to stretch his legs. He was on the main street of the town when his legs suddenly gave way and he collapsed. The strain of the long drive from Peking had caught up with him with no warning. He had simply fainted from fatigue.

Prince Scipione Borghese regained consciousness in the local jail. The police had been called by one of the townspeople and they had assumed that the man lying in the street was drunk. He needed a shave and a bath and he didn't look at all respectable. Even more serious was the fact that he didn't look like a German.

The police and the other prisoners all had a good laugh when the Italian told them his story. They had never heard of the Peking to Paris race. None of them believed that such a thing was possible. Neither did they believe that the unwashed and unshaven man in the cell was an Italian prince. He obviously wasn't Chinese either. The sergeant finally decided that Prince Borghese was crazy as well as drunk, so he told one of his men to handcuff him.

The Itala's mechanic got the surprise of his life when he came to the jail later that day to report the missing prince to the police.

The Prince, Paris— and Pons

At three in the afternoon of August 10, 1907, the Itala reached the suburbs of Paris. It seemed that every car owner in the city was there to welcome the winner. Every driver wanted to be a part of the triumphal entry. Crowds of excited people thronged the streets, shouting and throwing flowers into the Itala.

Prince Borghese and his mechanic sat proudly on their packing cases and waved to their cheering admirers. It had been a long, hard trip, but they had proved to the world that a car could do what many people would not have believed possible.

And the two De Dions and the Spyker also proved it. Although they arrived three weeks after Prince Borghese and his Itala, they all completed the long trip from Peking to Paris.

Only poor Augustin Pons and his tricycle had failed to make it all the way.

(5)

THE MADDEST, MOST AMBITIOUS RACE OF ALL TIME

It seems strange that the longest, toughest race in motoring history was run way back in 1908. There have been some spectacular events since that time, of course, but there has been nothing to top the race from New York to Paris. Even today such a trip would be looked upon as a great adventure.

Cars at that time were notoriously unreliable. Motors would suddenly sputter and die for no apparent reason. Something was always going wrong and the driver had to know how to put it right. He was often unable to phone a garage because there might not be one within a radius of 100 miles (160 km). Besides, there probably wasn't a phone handy anyway. The driver had to solve his own problems and most cars had a large box of tools and spare parts bolted to the running board. If the driver didn't know how to use them, he was out of luck.

Changing a tire today is a very simple procedure. Many drivers, in fact, have never had to change one. In 1908, however, flat tires were almost daily occurrences for car owners. A rock could easily punch a hole in the casing and fixing a tire in those days was terribly hard work. Flat tires were so common then that some cars had three or four spares lashed to the back.

In spite of the difficulties of long-distance travel by car, the idea of a race from New York to Paris appealed to a few hardy adventurers. They knew that it would be a tough trip, but they liked the challenge. They also liked the fact that they would be making motoring history.

The sponsors of the race must have taken a fiendish delight in planning the route. Their original plan called for the entries to cross the North American continent, then travel by steamer from Seattle to Alaska. The Alaskan part of the race was particularly interesting. After driving down frozen rivers to the Bering Strait, the cars would cross the ice to Russia and keep on going until they finally reached Paris. The total distance was just a little more than 13,000 miles (20,800 km) and there were even some fairly good roads in a few places.

Pons Again—and Paris

Six cars and their teams were lined up in front of *The New York Times* Building on the morning of February 12, 1908. There was one entry each from the United States, Germany, and Italy. The French, however, had entered three vehicles. They were a De Dion, a Motobloc, and a Sizaire-Naudin.

The Sizaire-Naudin was a tiny one-cylinder contraption piloted by none other than Augustin Pons, who had entered a tricycle in the Peking to Paris race the year before. Pons was now convinced that cars with four wheels were the answer. He refused to take any bets, but he boasted loudly that he would be the first one to get to Paris.

And he proved to be right! Things didn't turn out quite as he had planned, though. While the other cars were racing toward the Pacific, Pons was returning home across the Atlantic with his crippled car. When the remaining entries reached Paris several months later, Augustin Pons was there to welcome them.

The De Dion carried a very interesting store of emergency supplies. In addition to the usual things, it had a set of skis. These were to be used in place of the front wheels if the team ran into deep snow. They were also prepared for ice and had a set of wheels covered with steel studs. Perhaps the most novel piece of equipment aboard the De Dion was a mast and sail. The crew hoped that strong winds would help to speed them on their way and help to save fuel at the same time.

All of the cars had wheels which were designed especially for driving down rail line tracks. The crews would push their cars onto the tracks and they would then go speeding along like a mini-train. Everyone expected to make good use of the Union Pacific and trans-Siberian rail lines.

It was exactly a quarter after eleven in the morning when an official of the American Automobile Club fired the shot that started the race. An immense crowd roared its best wishes and a brass band played a lusty rhythm as the cars began to roll up Broadway. Plans called for the contestants to reach Albany by sunset, but not a single one of them made it. As a matter of interest, Pons in his tiny one-cylinder Sizaire-Naudin never did make it to Albany.

Augustin Pons must surely be the unluckiest long-distance racing driver in history. His Contal tricycle collapsed after covering only 10 miles (16 km) of the Peking to Paris race. The following year, his Sizaire-Naudin was forced to drop out of the New York to Paris race after chugging along for a mere 36 miles (58 km). After these two colossal failures, Pons wisely decided to retire from long-distance car racing.

The Italians also got themselves into trouble shortly after the start of the race. Their big Zust frightened a horse and an angry farmer refused to let them pass. Two policemen soon arrived on the scene. They decided that the car had done five dollars worth of damage to the horse. This apparently made sense to the Italians and they went speeding off after paying their debt.

Over: *the Thomas Flyer chugs through snow on the first leg of the race from New York to Paris. This was perhaps the greatest motoring epic of all time.*

Deep snow, bitter cold, and mechanical failures plagued the contestants on their journey through New York State. Mechanical failures and gooey mud plagued them throughout the Middle West. By the time the teams reached Iowa, only four cars were still in the picture. The Frenchmen driving the Motobloc were forced to retire for the very good reason that they had run out of money.

The Thomas Flyer, the American entry, led the other cars across the Great Plains and into the western states. Roads were practically nonexistent. In fact, the contestants thought they were lucky when they found wagon trails which were leading in their direction.

George Schuster, driver of the Thomas Flyer, decided that he could make better time on the railroad tracks. He politely asked the Union Pacific for their permission to use them and was politely told that the tracks were for trains. The Union Pacific was a very reasonable outfit, though. They officially made the Thomas Flyer a train and said that it was free to use the tracks at any time.

Unfortunately, this wasn't quite as great as it might sound. Bumping along over the wooden ties was grueling. Everything in the car was shaken loose and one burst tire followed another. Trains were an everpresent danger and the Flyer sometimes had to be manhandled off the tracks at very short notice.

A Swift Sojourn
to
Alaska and Back

Once the great barrier of the Rocky Mountains was behind them, the way to the Pacific seemed clear. The Americans made good time across the desert regions of Nevada and California and rolled into San Francisco on March 24. They had covered 3,800 miles (6,100 km) in forty-two days and were well in the lead. The Italian Zust was still battling its way across Utah. The French De Dion and the Germans in their Protos were way back in Wyoming.

After the Thomas Flyer had been completely overhauled, it was put on board a freighter for Alaska. The team landed in Valdez on April 8 and Schuster's worst fears were realized: The man who had dreamed up the Alaskan leg of the journey simply hadn't known what he was doing. There was no way on earth that a car could be driven across the vast wilderness area beyond Valdez.

Schuster described the situation in a telegram to the race officials in New York and asked for instructions. He was told to take a ship to Seattle, then take another one from there to the Russian port of Vladivostok.

The Thomas Flyer had never even been driven off the dock in Valdez, Alaska.

(6)
AND SO-ON TO SIBERIA

All the news waiting for the Americans in Seattle was bad. The Zust and De Dion had arrived in the city while the Thomas Flyer was in Alaska. The French and Italian teams knew that the race rules had been changed and had immediately set off for Vladivostok.

Meanwhile, the German racers appeared in Seattle. They didn't appear under their own steam, however. Their Protos had broken down in Utah. They weren't able to get it repaired there, so they had shipped it to the coast on a freight train.

The American team didn't like the situation at all. It almost seemed as though they were being penalized for reaching the coast first. While they were sitting in Seattle, the De Dion and the Zust were steaming toward Asia. Although the Thomas Flyer was actually leading the race, it was hundreds of miles behind the French and Italian cars.

George Schuster was particularly concerned about the Germans. They had broken one of the major rules of the race by shipping their Protos to Seattle. Schuster did not want the team to be disqualified, but he didn't want them to have any unfair advantages either.

Race officials soon solved the problem. They ruled that if the Germans reached Paris, fifteen extra days would be added to their driving time. In the case of the Americans, fifteen days would be subtracted from their time if they managed to finish the journey. Everyone accepted this and the two teams soon left Seattle for Russia.

Just about the first thing they heard in Vladivostok was that the De Dion had dropped out of the race. Their financial supporter in Paris had simply said that no more money would be forthcoming and that was that. It was impossible to carry on without money, so the poor French were forced to give up.

The Italians were also having more than their share of problems. They had the bad luck to be crossing a river in Manchuria when they were hit by a flash flood. The team managed to swim to the safety of some high ground, but the big Zust was never again quite the same after its stay under water. Although they had almost no chance of winning, the team decided to remain in the race anyway. After all, they' had to get back to Italy somehow.

Hello and a Quick
Good-bye to Kiakhta

Spring was simply the wrong time of the year to be racing a car across Asia. Heavy rains and melting snows turned quiet little rivers into raging floods. The countryside in many places was a sea of mud. On several occasions, Schuster had to wait for the flood waters to recede, then found that the mud left in its wake made further progress almost impossibly difficult.

Whenever it was practical, the Thomas Flyer was put on the tracks of the trans-Siberian rail line. Although this was a terribly uncomfortable way to travel, it was better than being stuck in the mud.

A welcome the Americans received in a village in western Siberia was particularly interesting. They were just passing the first house when a woman rushed out and hurled an egg straight at partner Linn Mathewson's left eye. Someone from virtually every house in the village ran out to wage war. Before the Thomas Flyer reached the safety of the Siberian countryside, the two men had been pelted with mud, apples, more eggs, and approximately three bushels of potatoes.

They later learned the reason for the strange behavior. While racing through the village the previous day, the German team had run over someone's goat. That was the first time that any of the villagers had seen a car, but they now looked upon every car in the world as their enemy.

The Americans' welcome in the central Siberian city of Kiakhta was an entirely different story. This was the home of some enormously rich businessmen who were determined to show the racers a good time. They were so determined, in fact, that Schuster and Mathewson could hardly get out of town fast enough.

The party got underway as soon as the Thomas Flyer came rolling into town. Although it was still quite early in the morning, bottles of champagne and vodka were thrust at them from every direction. Toasts had to be drunk to just about everything imaginable. The two men were then escorted to one of the local night clubs. Women plied them with food and drink while laughing Siberians pounded them on the back and proposed one toast after another.

This was exactly the last thing Schuster and Mathewson had wanted. Both of them were filthy dirty and tired. For days on end, they had been hauling the Thomas Flyer across rivers, sand traps, and sinks of mud. They had changed more tires then they cared to remember and spent many hours working on a balky engine. Both of them were in need of a hot bath and a good night's sleep. They had hoped to get them in Kiakhta, but the chances of that now seemed remote.

As things turned out, the Thomas Flyer would not have spent much time in Kiakhta anyway. While the American drivers were reluctantly drinking toasts with their Siberian hosts, a policeman came charging up and told them that another car had just driven through town. The Americans knew that it could only be the German Protos and they decided to set off at once.

It seemed that everyone in town had a farewell gift for them. Schuster told their new friends that their car was already loaded to capacity, but nobody listened. Presents of food and drink were shoved into any spot that would hold them. Mathewson was holding a leg of lamb on his lap when the Thomas Flyer went chugging west out of Kiakhta.

An American Victory

Ever since leaving Vladivostok, the lead had seesawed back and forth between the Germans and the Americans. The Thomas Flyer was a faster car than the Protos, but bad luck hounded Mathewson and Schuster.

In spite of their best efforts, the Germans' lead became more substantial every day. Unless something unforeseen happened, the Protos would beat the Flyer to Paris. The thought of this happening terrified Schuster. Getting to Paris first had become the single most important thing in his life.

The Americans got the bad news when they reached Berlin on July 26. The Protos had rolled into Paris the day before. This didn't mean, though, that they had won the race. Because of the fifteen-day penalty they had received for shipping their car from Utah to Seattle, they were officially two full weeks behind the Thomas Flyer.

At exactly eight in the evening of July 30, 1908, the American team drove up to the *Le Matin* Building in Paris. Although they unfortunately hadn't gotten there first, the weary racers were welcomed as the winners. They had driven 13,341 miles (21,479 km) in 169 days.

The original thought behind the New York to Paris race had been to test the toughness of the motor car. It proved more than that, however. It proved, too, that the toughness of the car depended to a great degree upon the courage, stamina, and ingenuity of the drivers.

But we can't forget the brave and determined Italian team. They had run into every problem imaginable in their backbreaking trip from Vladivostok. The Zust had been pulled out of sand and mud by camels, mules, horses, and men of a dozen different nationalities. Broken parts for the car had been rebuilt in remote villages in Mongolia and Siberia. Constant stomach upsets plagued the Italians and they were almost driven mad by infected insect bites. They refused to give up, however, and they made it!

Just fifty days after the American team had been declared the winner of the New York to Paris race, the Italian team came rolling into the city.

Unfortunately, no brass band or cheering crowd was there to welcome them.

(7)
LE MANS

The race held every June in Le Mans, France is a twenty-four-hour affair. It was held for the first time in 1923 and it has been called many things since then. It has been called a super spectacular, a stinker, a murder marathon, and an endurance derby.

The rules of the race are really quite simple. Cars are divided into four classes according to engine size. The car which has covered the most miles after twenty-four hours of nonstop speeding is the winner in its class. A driver can change places with his partner whenever he feels like it.

Some drivers say that Le Mans is the toughest race of them all and maybe it is. There is simply no time to relax and look around. The course covers just under 8½ miles (13.5 km) and absolute concentration is required every step of the way. This is actually more difficult than it sounds because the drivers are apt to get a bit "road happy" after driving round and round for hour after hour at top speed.

Perhaps the most dramatic case of road happiness was recorded at Le Mans in 1952. Pierre Levegh, a Frenchman driving a French Talbot, was leading the race at six in the morning. He had been driving nonstop for fourteen hours and there were still ten more hours to go. Although he was getting very tired, he refused to let René Marchand, his partner, take over.

Levegh drove on and on, refusing to spare either himself or the car. He was like a man possessed. His face had taken on a greenish hue, his eyes were glassy, and his hands shook. He could neither eat nor drink. Even talking became difficult. And yet he refused to give up his place behind the wheel.

After twenty straight hours of nerve-racking racing at breakneck speed, Levegh was practically in a state of collapse. His friends and mechanics at the pit stops begged him to let Marchand drive for at least an hour, but there was just no way to reason with the racer.

Less than two hours of the twenty-four remained when Levegh made his last pit stop. He had been driving at nearly 100 miles (160 km) an hour for over twenty-two hours. Although he was well in the lead, he was paying a heavy price for his stubbornness. He was so far gone that he no longer knew what people were saying to him.

As the Le Mans entered its twenty-fourth and final hour, the pit crew made desperate attempts to get through to Levegh. He was 25 miles (40 km) ahead of the car in second place. If he slowed down to 50 miles (80 km) an hour, he would spare himself and the car and still win the race. Levegh, though, was too far gone by this time to heed the advice. The race was almost over and he was going to finish at top speed.

Unfortunately, the race ended for Pierre Levegh while there were still thirty-four minutes to go. A broken crankshaft put him out of the running. He had driven 2,321 miles (3,737 km) in twenty-three hours and twenty-six minutes and he had been in the lead almost all of that time.

When Levegh was told that he would not be able to finish the race, he broke down and wept. Victory could hardly have been closer.

A Long, Sad Day in France

Although American drivers and American cars have put on many good shows at Le Mans in recent years, they didn't do too well in the early days. Their first year there, in fact, was a real tearjerker.

In 1926, the Americans arrived in Le Mans with three entries for the race. One was a Willys-Knight; the other two were Overlands. Mechanics got the cars into peak racing condition and the drivers then took off to get the feel of the course.

The driver of one of the Overlands got a very bad feel indeed. Somehow or another he managed to shoot off the road and smash into a tree. The car was damaged beyond repair and the driver was nowhere to be found.

It wasn't until a week later that an enterprising reporter found the driver in a seedy hotel in Le Havre. The American had booked passage on a ship to New York and stubbornly refused to discuss the accident with anyone. To this day, nobody knows how an experienced racing driver was able to miss a gentle curve and run smack into the only tree in sight.

Although the Willys-Knight fell by the wayside early in the race, the second Overland put on a rather interesting show. It could only win, though, if every other car in the race broke down. The Overland was game, but the poor thing kept falling farther and farther behind. There was just no way that the American car could maintain the speeds averaged by the French, German, Italian, and British entries. Finally, after more than twenty-two hours of heroic struggling, the gallant Overland lay down and died of an oil leak.

Certainly the most interesting car ever entered at Le Mans was an American Duesenberg owned by Prince Nicholas of Romania. This beautiful car had absolutely no chance of winning. It was huge and heavy and had not been built for speed.

The Duesenberg was the kind of car you would expect a prince to own. Movie stars also liked Duesenbergs and so did Arab sheiks, Indian maharajas, and millionaire playboys. And when there was a procession for a visiting dignitary, the lead car was sometimes a Duesenberg.

The crowd at Le Mans normally cheered only the French cars and French drivers. They all loved the lovely big Duesenberg, however. Prince Nicholas would always wave cheerfully when he came racing past the grandstand and there would always be a roar of delight. He even honked his horn a time or two and the crowd loved it.

For nearly two hours, Prince Nicholas came whizzing grandly past the grandstand at regular eight-minute intervals. But then something went wrong. Nine minutes passed, then ten, then fifteen, and then twenty. And still no Prince Nicholas and no Duesenberg. Finally, the sad story was announced over the loudspeaker. Poor Prince Nicholas of Romania had run out of gas on the Arnage Curve.

The only American car entered in the 1933 Le Mans Super Spectacular had fallen by the wayside and Prince Nicholas had a very red face.

(8)
THE INDIANAPOLIS SPEEDWAY

In 1908, four businessmen in Indianapolis put their heads together and decided to build the biggest and best testing ground for cars that the world had ever known. The testing ground would include a race track and races would be held every year. This was a novel idea because many people living in Indianapolis at that time had never even seen a car.

The Indianapolis Speedway—as an imaginative newspaperman called it—was finished in July, 1909. A series of events was scheduled for the following month. This included motorcycle racing as well as car racing. There was even a balloon race thrown in for good measure. The main event, however, was to be held on the third and final day. This was to be a 300-mile (480 km) race around the 2½-mile (4 km) track.

The troubles started almost at once. The surface of the track was a mixture of crushed rock and tar. Although it looked fine, it couldn't stand the strain of heavy cars pounding over it at top speed. A layer of loose grit formed and the speeding cars went into some very spectacular skids. Conditions soon became so bad that the officials had to stop the race.

Over: *cars enter the first turn in the initial Indy 500 in May 1911.*

It was obvious that the track's surface had to be changed and the best engineers were called in. They decided that bricks laid in cement were the answer. An order was placed for 3,200,000 bricks and the job was finished early in 1910.

The racing events of 1910 were not financially rewarding. People were still annoyed that the race had been stopped the year before. They felt that they hadn't gotten their money's worth and that was a serious matter. Nobody likes to feel that he's been cheated.

As a matter of fact, the owners and drivers weren't too happy about the Speedway in 1910 either. The poor attendance was costing the owners piles of money; the drivers didn't like the new brick surface. They said it was so rough and bumpy that it practically shook the fillings out of their teeth.

It was apparent that some changes still had to be made and the four owners once again put their heads together. Solving the problems of the track's surface was not too difficult. They simply had a contractor smooth it over with asphalt.

The other changes involved the series of events put on at the Speedway. The people wanted something really spectacular and the owners decided to give them what they wanted. They decided to make the Indianapolis Speedway the race track that everyone talked about. There would be only one race a year, but what a race it would be!

The race that was dreamed up by those men in 1910 became the Indianapolis 500 and is still run every year on Memorial Day.

Heartbreak and a Hero

May 30, 1911 was a lovely day for a car race. In spite of the fact that the cost of tickets had gone way up, a crowd of almost one hundred thousand people came to see the first Indianapolis 500. They had come looking for thrills and they weren't disappointed. There was enough excitement that day to please everyone.

Drivers had arrived in Indianapolis from all over the United States and from several European countries. Like the knights of old, they were seeking fame and fortune. The driver who won the 500 would be a big hero. He would also be a rather rich man. The first prize was $10,000. That may not sound like such a big deal now, but a worker who brought home two dollars a day in 1911 looked upon himself as quite successful.

The make of many of the cars entered in the first Indy 500 sound very strange to us today. They include such long-forgotten names as Simplex, Inter State, Pope Hartford, National, Cutting, and Amplex. There were also three Cases entered by the J.I. Case Threshing Machine Company of Racine, Wisconsin. And, believe it or not, a Buick was entered by a man named Arthur Chevrolet.

Ray Harroun, a young New Yorker, won the first 500 in a Marmon Wasp. It had taken him six hours and forty minutes to do the 200 laps. His average speed had been 75 miles (120 km) an hour. The winner of the second prize was only a minute behind Harroun.

The second Indianapolis 500 was even more exciting than the first. There were enough crashes to please everyone. There was also a bit of heartbreak and drama that is still talked about in racing circles today.

Ralph de Palma, a twenty-one-year-old American driving a big German Mercedes-Benz, looked like a cinch to win the 1912 Indy. At the end of the 197th lap, he was 10 miles (16 km) ahead of Joe Dawson, his nearest rival. All he had to do was to maintain his lead for three more laps and he would be the winner. The big fat first prize which had shot up to 15,000 beautiful dollars from the year before would be all his.

But fate wasn't smiling on popular young Ralph de Palma that sunny spring afternoon in 1912. His engine started making very nasty clanking sounds early in the 198th lap. The clanks got louder and louder and poor de Palma became

Over: *Ray Harroun won the first Indy 500 with an average speed of 75 miles (120 km) an hour.*

(51)

unhappier and unhappier. The oil pressure was dropping fast and the car was losing speed. Something had gone terribly wrong.

The big Mercedes-Benz choked, sputtered, and clanked its way into the 200th lap. Oil pressure had dropped to zero. The engine noise was awful. The car jerked and chugged forward at little more than a snail's pace. Dawson saw that de Palma was in big trouble and he drove even faster than before.

The finish line was in sight when the Mercedes finally gave its last clank and stopped dead in its tracks. But Ralph de Palma was not the kind of man who gave up easily. Jumping out of the car, he began pushing it toward the man with the checkered flag. The Mercedes, though, was a very heavy machine and he was barely able to inch it along. Joe Dawson waved sympathetically as he shot past the unlucky de Palma on his final lap and went on to collect his $15,000 prize.

Although Ralph de Palma did not win the Indianapolis 500 of 1912, he won a place in the history of the Speedway. More than one hundred thousand people cheered themselves hoarse when de Palma pushed his stricken car across the finish line.

There have been many dramatic Memorial Days at Indianapolis since that time, but Ralph de Palma's courage and will to win will always be remembered.

Janet Guthrie

Janet Guthrie is another name that will always be remembered at Indianapolis. Why? Because Janet is a woman and, before her, no woman had ever even attempted to drive in the Indy 500.

No one dared suggest, of course, that women could not drive as well as men. That idea had been knocked in the head as early as 1903 when Marie du Gast performed so admirably in the Paris to Madrid event. Since that time, many women had proved themselves in races the world over.

The Indy, though, was different, the critics insisted. These cars were not conventional automobiles. They were turbo-charged monsters with so much horsepower that they zoomed along like rockets. They were simply too big and powerful for a woman to handle. Especially if the woman happened to weigh only 135 pounds (61 kg).

Janet arrived in Indianapolis on May 8, 1976. Her rookie tests were scheduled for May 11. This meant circling the track twenty times at an average speed of 160 miles (258 km) an hour. She then had to repeat the performance averaging 165 miles (266 km) an hour.

The rookie tests were a great success. The next step was to get out on the track and hit 180 (290). If she could manage that, Janet would have an excellent chance of being one of the thirty-three drivers to qualify for the 1976 Indy 500.

Even her most severe critics had to sing her praises. Janet failed to qualify through no fault of her own. She drove flawlessly, but her Bryant Special refused to cooperate. The car was temperamental and she simply could not coax it up to the 180 (290) mark. Rules are rules and the judges had no choice. There was no place in the 1976 Indy 500 for the unlucky Janet Guthrie.

But 1977 was a new year. Early in May, Janet showed up in Indianapolis with a newer and more powerful car. She took her rookie tests, and speeds of well over 180 miles (290 km) an hour qualified her for the 500 and a dream had come true.

The fact that Janet Guthrie did not win the race is not important. She had proved to the world that a woman could compete successfully in one of the toughest and most demanding sporting events on earth. By doing so, she had won the respect and admiration of the best racing drivers in the game.

(9)
A BEACH
CALLED DAYTONA

Sometime during the summer of 1870, a man named Mathias Day found an area south of Jacksonville, Florida that impressed him greatly. It was his idea of a tropical paradise. Breezes from the Atlantic kept the sunny days from getting too hot. The water was warm and a beach of hard-packed white sand stretched for miles and miles. Day was so impressed with the place that he laid out the plans for a city and modestly called it Day Town.

The climate attracted wealthy, sun-seeking Northerners as well as a certain number of penniless beach bums. The two different groups did, however, have one thing in common: They insisted upon calling their new home Daytona Beach.

It was the Automobile Age that really put Daytona Beach on the map. The long, flat stretch of white sand was just perfect for racing. Wealthy residents boasted cheerfully of achieving speeds of 20 and even 25 miles (32 to 40 km) an hour in their new cars. Word of the ideal racing conditions on the Florida beach spread rapidly and enthusiasts from the northern cities came chugging south. By 1900, Daytona Beach thought of itself as America's Speed Capital.

The question of speed intrigued a young millionaire from Scotland. He wanted to know how fast a car could really go and he was willing to pay a lot of money to find out. The conditions were perfectly clear and simple: The man who could drive a measured mile in the shortest time would win "The Thomas Dewar Cup" and a big cash prize.

Racing drivers from all over the world gathered at Daytona Beach in January 1905. Alex Winton, Barney Oldfield, and Henry Ford, America's most famous racers, were all ready and eager to go. Louis Ross, a racer hardly anyone had ever heard of, was also ready and eager to go.

Ross had been hired by the Stanley twins, Francis Edgar and Freelan Oscar, to race the steam car they had built. The brothers called their car a "Wogglebug," but everyone else called it a "Stanley Steamer." A reporter said that it looked like an upside-down canoe and that description was actually quite a good one.

The spectators chuckled happily when Louis Ross went wheezing and puffing off down the beach in his funny little car. Henry Ford and the other drivers had gone well past the starting line to get up as much speed as possible. Ross, however, disappeared completely from sight. He wanted to get up a good head of steam before reaching the starting line. It took him a couple of miles to really get going, but very few people knew that.

A little ripple of mirth ran through the crowd when the Stanley Steamer appeared in the distance. Their laughter, however, soon became a gasp of astonishment. Ross was tearing along at an incredible rate. He was almost flying over the sand when he passed the officials.

Neither the officials nor the spectators could believe what they were seeing. Not even in their wildest dreams would they have thought that a Stanley Steamer was capable of such speed. The officials checked and rechecked their stop watches and they knew that they couldn't have made a mistake. Louis Ross had covered the measured mile in exactly thirty-eight seconds.

This meant, then, that he had been driving at an average speed of 94.7 miles (152 km) per hour.

The Race That Couldn't Keep Going

Breaking speed records was a lot of fun, but the city fathers wanted to attract more people to Daytona Beach. More people meant more money and that was something the city needed badly. Perhaps, someone suggested, a really spectacular car race might solve their problem.

That seemed like a good suggestion. Racing had become a very popular sport and Daytona Beach was an ideal spot for such an event. The city fathers quickly gave the idea their blessing and the city's most respected racing driver was put in charge of the operation.

The racer went right straight to work. The track was his first concern, of course, and his plan was a wonderfully simple one. It was also a very, very inexpensive one. A blacktop road ran parallel to the beach. All he had to do was to measure off 1.5 miles (2.4 km) of both the beach and road. He would then join them together by cutting two U-shaped roads through the sand dunes. This would give him a very nice little oval race track.

The big event was scheduled for March 8, 1936. Well before that date, drivers from Latin America, Europe, and all over the United States began arriving in Daytona Beach. They had come for the thrills and the biggest thrill of all would be winning some of the $5000 that was to be given away in prize money.

It's not unusual for a racing driver to become a millionaire today, but that wasn't the case then. The United States was going through the worst depression in its history in 1936 and even $1000 was considered a fortune.

Officials had decided that the race was to cover 250 miles (400 km). This was just a bit more than seventy-eight laps around the track. That should be enough to please even the most demanding enthusiast, the officials reasoned. The crowd would get its money's worth and everyone would go home happy.

Unfortunately, things didn't work out quite that way. The first signs of trouble came soon after the race got started. Wilbur Erdmann, a Wisconsin driver, got stuck in one of the stretches of sand connecting the beach and the blacktop road. While Erdmann was being towed out, another driver got stuck on the opposite end of the track.

Events soon reached ridiculous proportions. Drivers charged down the beach at full throttle, then bogged down helplessly on the connecting roads. And there they fidgeted unhappily until the tow truck came to their rescue. As soon as they had been pulled free, they raced off toward the next stretch of sand where they got stuck again.

The poor overworked tow truck simply could not cope. Only one vehicle at a time could be rescued and there were times when two or three cars were all stuck at once. An urgent call was made for a second tow truck and it came rushing straight out to the track. A minute later, it was stuck tightly in the sand. Even some of the racers managed a small smile when they saw one tow truck towing the other tow truck out to the road.

It was obvious to the officials that something had to be done. The race was no longer a race. Getting around the track without getting stuck had simply become a matter of luck. There was really no sense in driving at top speed along a blacktop road if you were going to get stuck in a sand dune immediately afterwards. The officials sadly concluded that there was only one thing they could do: They would have to stop the race.

Daytona Comes of Age

The unfortunate events of 1936 never occurred again. After the horrible foul-up of that year, the organizers went to great lengths to see that everything went smoothly. Drivers enjoyed racing at Daytona and some of the best in the world came to race over the sands. Fans flocked in from hundreds of miles away and a steady stream of money flowed into the city.

Things were going well, but an enthusiastic promoter named Bill France thought that they could go even better. He began talking about building a super-speedway at Daytona Beach. The main race would cover 500 miles (800 km) and be run in February. Florida was full of tourists at that time of the year and masses of them would pay good money to see a good race.

Not everyone thought that Bill France's idea was a good one. Some said that Daytona Beach couldn't afford a super-speedway. Others said that tourists came to Florida for the sun and they wouldn't leave the beach to go to a race track. Still others insisted that Daytona Beach would never be able to compete with Indianapolis.

In spite of the gloomy predictions of the scoffers, Bill France got his speedway. The first 500-mile (800 km) race was run on February 22, 1959 and it was a roaring success. The bleachers were full to overflowing and the crowd spilled over onto the beach.

Some interesting figures emerged from the two main races of 1959. Lee Petty, winner of the Daytona 500, had averaged 135.5 miles (218 km) an hour. The winner of the Indianapolis 500 had averaged 135.8 miles (218.4 km) an hour—a mere .3 miles (.4 km) an hour faster than the Daytona winner. Daytona fans were jubilant, but the fans in Indianapolis tried to act as though the Daytona 500 had never happened.

Daytona Beach, however, stubbornly refused to go away. As soon as a record was set at Indianapolis, it was either matched or beaten in Florida. This went on year after year.

Then a young American named Mario Andretti delivered the crushing blow. Although it was known that Andretti had won the Daytona 500, Indy fans were not impressed. Racing at Daytona was one thing; racing at Indianapolis was something else. Besides, Andretti didn't even look like a racing driver. He was so short that he could barely see over the steering wheel. Surely a man like that could not possibly win a *real* race, the Indy fans told one another.

But the mighty Indy 500 was won in 1969 by a little man named Mario Andretti. Not only did Andretti win the race, he won it at the bruising speed of 156.9 miles (252.4 km) an hour. He had learned his lesson well at Daytona.

Racing fans in Indianapolis now admit that Daytona Beach is here to stay. They resent the fact, though, that the Florida city calls itself the "World Center of Racing." That name, they insist, belongs to Indianapolis and to Indianapolis only.

Daytona, Indianapolis, and
the American Automobile

In 1901, Gordon Bennett publicly lamented the fact that Americans didn't seem to be very interested in cars or racing. What a surprise there would be in store for him if he could attend a Daytona 500 or an Indianapolis 500 today! He might even have trouble finding an empty seat in the grandstand.

Until recently, Americans were known for their love of big, shiny automobiles, complete with automatic windows, air conditioning, and cruise control features. But the energy shortage has had a marked effect on Americans' attitudes toward cars.

More and more drivers are switching from huge gas guzzlers to smaller models. People no longer boast about getting only 10 miles (16 km) to the gallon (4 l) in their big Buicks. They now boast about getting 30 miles (48 km) to the gallon (4 l) in their four-cylinder, front-wheel drive subcompacts.

In spite of all the problems, millions of Americans are still very interested in cars and racing today. These are subjects almost everyone enjoys discussing.

Gordon Bennett would be proud of us.

(10)

THE COUNTRY THAT SUDDENLY BECOMES A RACE TRACK

"You don't have to be crazy to race in Monaco," declared Jack Brabham, "but it certainly does help."

Brabham was quite right. The Monaco Grand Prix is the craziest event in big-time racing. There is no race track, so the fast and powerful cars go tearing through the narrow, twisting streets of the city.

One complete lap measures just under 2 miles (3 km) and there's a very good reason for that: The tiny principality of Monaco is simply not large enough to accommodate anything more ambitious. The country is so small that a child on a bicycle could pedal across the whole place in a matter of minutes. The total area of the Principality of Monaco is just exactly 368 acres (147 hectares). This is roughly the same size as a large dairy farm in the Middle West.

Everyone in Monaco wants to see the race. So do many thousands of others who come flooding into town. Every window along the route is full of faces. Every tree is full of men and children. There are people perched on rooftops and squatting on walls. There are also people bobbing about on yachts and small boats in the harbor. They have all come to see the action and there's always plenty of that in the Monaco Grand Prix.

Make No Mistakes in Monaco
It's hard to believe that one of the world's most important annual car races is run in Monaco. As far as racing is concerned,

everything about the place seems to be wrong. There is no country driving at all because Monaco has no countryside. The only straight stretch in the entire race is less than .5 miles (.8 km) long.

Almost everything in Monaco is either uphill or downhill. The royal palace is situated on a high escarpment and the country slopes steeply down to the harbor from there. The world-famous gambling casino of Monte Carlo is high on the hillside and wealthy tourists can peer through the Edwardian windows at the racers roaring past.

There is simply no margin for error at Monaco. "You don't even dare blink your eyes or you may find yourself in somebody's livingroom," quipped one driver. To keep this from happening, many residents pile high rows of sandbags in front of their doors and windows. They don't want any uninvited guests dropping in on them from the street outside. And especially not if the guests bring their cars in with them.

This actually happened during the 1936 Grand Prix. A driver misjudged a corner while moving along as fast as he dared to go. His car bounced off the curb, then went sailing through the warm Mediterranean afternoon. Car and driver sailed straight through a heavy wooden door and came to a sudden stop against a large stone fireplace.

Unfortunately, the lady of the house was one of the very few people in Monaco who had no interest in racing. To make matters worse, her uninvited guest was a German. Germany was preparing for war in 1936 and she was afraid of what might happen in Europe. It would never do to have a citizen of an enemy country in her house, she decided, so she told the stunned and surprised German to take his car and get out of her living room as fast as he could.

Alberto Ascari, a racer who won the World Championship in 1952 and 1953, also performed a spectacular aerial act at Monaco. He skidded on Harbor Road, went out of control, and shot off into the blue. The Lancia flew over a cabin cruiser riding at anchor in the harbor and dived into the Mediterranean with a great splash and a hiss of steam.

A few seconds later, Ascari popped to the surface and began swimming toward shore with strong, sure strokes. And he was still wearing his blue crash helmet! Perhaps, someone suggested later, he was afraid that another car might land on his head.

Time Out for Coca Cola

The accident rate at Monaco is awesome to say the least. It's all up and down. The road is often no more than 20 feet (6 m) wide. Although a lap is just a fraction under 2 miles (about 3 km), there are ten very sharp corners that have to be maneuvered on each lap. The Grand Prix consists of 100 laps and that means 1,000 sharp corners, some taken at speeds of 100 miles (160 km) an hour. To make matters even more interesting, every driver is trying his best to pass everyone else.

Passing another car on the narrow twisting streets of Monaco is a terribly tricky business. A driver has to take certain risks to win the race, but the tiniest miscalculation can spell disaster. Louis Chiron learned this to his sorrow when he tried to pass Rudolf Caracciola during one of the early Grand Prix.

Rudolf Caracciola was a man with a problem. People could not pronounce his name, so everyone called him Coca Cola. Caracciola had absolutely no sense of humor. He hated his nickname, but there was just nothing at all that he could do about it. Even the racing officials knew him as Coca Cola and gleeful shouts of "Come on, Coca Cola!" often came from the crowd.

Caracciola may have been a very glum individual, but he was an excellent racing driver. He had won several major races and was leading the field at Monaco when Chiron came up behind him. Chiron was desperately anxious to get past. That would put him in the lead position and he was convinced that he could win the race if only he could squeeze past Coca Cola in his Mercedes-Benz.

The race was still in its early stages when Chiron thought he saw his chance. Caracciola slacked off just a fraction on a particularly sharp corner. Chiron shot forward in his Bugatti, but the gap was just not wide enough. The car clipped a barrier and spun out of control.

It was still spinning when an Alfa Romeo and a Ferrari came roaring around the corner. There was no time to take any avoiding action. Before the officials were able to warn the oncoming drivers, a total of five cars were out of business.

Because of the conditions at Monaco, only sixteen cars actually enter the Grand Prix. Many of these are eliminated very early in the race. This was illustrated most dramatically in the Monaco Grand Prix of 1950.

It was a beautiful day in May. Some of the best drivers in the world were taking part in the race and they were driving some of the world's most powerful and expensive cars. An official stepped forward with his checkered flag and the great crowd of spectators fell silent. The race was about to begin.

The sixteen cars got off to a flying start. For the first minute or so, in fact, it looked like a speeding traffic jam. Then Juan Fangio—probably the greatest of all racing drivers—shot well into the lead in his Alfa Romeo. Giuseppe Farina, also driving an Alfa Romeo, forced his way through to second place.

It all happened early in lap two. Farina swerved to avoid a patch of oil, bounced off the wall, and lost control for a split second. That was all the time it took to kick off one of the biggest pileups in the history of Grand Prix racing.

Before Farina could get straightened out, José-Froilan Gonzales came screaming around the corner in a Maserati and smashed into him. But that was only the beginning. There was just no way to miss the stricken racers and one driver after another piled into Farina and Gonzales. Seconds later, nine smashed cars lay in a heap of twisted wreckage. The race was less than four minutes old, but more than half of the entries had already been wiped out.

That's not quite the end of it, though. There were no serious injuries at all and all of the nine drivers again drove in the Monaco Grand Prix.

(11)
THE RACE THAT NOBODY WON

Summer sometimes comes to England rather late. There are times, too, when summer doesn't seem to come at all. The British are always optimistic, however, and they were sure that May 5, 1951 would be a nice, sunny Saturday. It wasn't, but nobody can be blamed for that.

The event was the *Daily Express* British Racing Drivers Club International Trophy. The race would be over before anyone could say all that, so they simply called it the Silverstone. This is the name of the village next to the track. The name stuck and the race has been known as the Silverstone ever since.

Those who followed racing closely said that Giuseppe Farina was the man to watch. Farina was the unlucky Italian who had been driving the first car in the nine-car pileup at the Monaco Grand Prix the year before. His luck had changed greatly after that, though, and he had gone on to become the World Champion. Farina had impressed the crowd and the other drivers by setting a new lap record at Silverstone.

Another man to watch was Prince Birabongse of Thailand. He had no chance at all of winning the race unless all of the other drivers dropped dead. In spite of that slight handicap, it was fun to watch him anyway. His big car was black and shiny and so were his silk coveralls. He wore a shiny black silk scarf around his neck and even his hair was black and shiny.

As starting time approached, more and more people glanced nervously at the sky. A storm was also approaching and it looked like a real prizewinner. The rumble of thunder rolled closer and closer. One lightning flash after another ripped through the inky dark clouds. An icy wind seemed to be blowing in straight from the North Pole and over one hundred thousand sets of teeth chattered in the grandstand.

The scene on the track was one of frantic activity. Mechanics worked feverishly to get wet-weather tires on the cars, then stood staring at the approaching storm. There was no more they could do at the moment. Drivers exchanged their goggles for rain visors and pulled on rainproof jackets. They all knew that they had a really tough drive ahead of them.

There was a moment of calm just before the starter swung his flag. Then the storm struck in earnest. Even spectators sitting in the center of the grandstand were soaked by the driving rain. Reporters, radio commentators, and officials in the front rows tried desperately hard to keep their papers dry. Television crews muttered under their breath about the English weather as they ran for cover. Mechanics huddled miserably in the pits and wished that they were somewhere else.

Conditions got worse by the minute. Many of the spectators had never seen a storm like it. Although it was still early in the afternoon, it seemed more like night. Leaden black clouds hung low in the sky. Thunder rolled and rumbled across flat farmland. Shafts of forked lightning flashed in every direction.

Confusion soon became the order of the day. Cars racing past in the pelting rain were little more than a blur. Half of the cars were driving blindly through the spray kicked up by the cars in front of them. It took a lot of luck just to stay on the track.

The officials were having a particularly tough time. There was just no way for them to tell how the race was progressing because it was impossible to tell who was who. "That's Fangio," an official called out at one point as a blur went speeding past.

"Couldn't be," a second official objected. "Fangio is driving an Alfa Romeo."

"That *was* an Alfa Romeo," the first one insisted.

"Well, it looked like a Maserati to me," countered Number Two, then added quickly, "I wouldn't take any bets on it, though."

As bad as things were, they steadily got worse. The torrent of rain suddenly became a hammering hailstorm. Brakes were useless on the bed of hailstones blanketing the track. Cars skidded helplessly and collided with other cars which the drivers could not even see.

Reports reaching officials were very grim indeed. Drivers had no idea where they were in the order of the race. They didn't know whether they were in first place or last. Neither did they know where they were on the track. It was simply a case of racing on and hoping for the best.

Although they hated to do it, the officials knew that the race had to be stopped. The timekeepers, in fact, had already put their stop watches away. They couldn't tell who they were timing, so there was no sense in keeping time.

Stopping the race proved to be a tougher job than anyone would have thought. Most of the drivers raced straight past the flag without slowing down. Visibility was so bad that they hadn't even been able to see it. They had no way of knowing that time was no longer being kept, so they raced on through the storm as fast as they dared.

Several more officials came out onto the track and waved flags. Mechanics came out of the pits and waved anything they could get their hands on. Everyone, of course, was very, very careful. They knew that the drivers could hardly see a thing and they didn't want to get run over.

Drivers who were finally flagged to a stop were sorry to hear that the race had been stopped. They had come to Silverstone to win and now they had lost their chance of victory. It was sad, but it couldn't be helped. Much of the track had become a lake. Drivers were driving blind much of the time. A blinded driver could crash into the crowd and such a happening dared not be risked.

Ten minutes after the race had officially been stopped, two British drivers were still tearing madly around the track. They were Tony Holt and Reg Parnell. "Stop! Stop!" yelled the officials and mechanics. "Go! Go!" boomed thousands of voices from the grandstand.

Holt finally fell out with engine trouble and Parnell realized at long last that he was the only one left on the track. He was obviously annoyed when he pulled in at the pits. "What's wrong?" he yelled above the roar of the storm. "Why did you stop it?"

"Too dangerous," an official shouted through cupped hands. "You can't race in weather like this."

"I was having a lovely time," Parnell called, then added quickly, "So who won anyway?"

It was a question the official hadn't wanted to hear. Many had thought that Reg Parnell would win at Silverstone, but the weather had changed all that. According to international racing rules, there could not be a winner in an unfinished race.

(12)
THE RACE THAT ALMOST EVERYBODY WINS

"You can't win a race unless you finish it," Juan Fangio often said. The young man from Argentina certainly knew what he was talking about. He won the World Drivers Championship five times and retired from racing while he was still in one piece.

Fangio did not say that everyone who finished a race won the race. He merely said that you had to finish a race in order to win it. There is one race, however, in which every finisher is declared a winner. Another interesting feature of the race is the fact that there are no losers. This event is the London to Brighton Vintage Car Run.

The British describe the event as a "run" rather than a "race." This is probably a more accurate term. Very few races have any restrictions on speed, but the London to Brighton Run very definitely does. The speed limit today is 20 miles (32 km) an hour and it's considered very bad manners to drive any faster.

Another important restriction is the age of the entry. Only cars manufactured before December 31, 1904 are eligible. Now, 1904 is a long time ago. It's rather hard to believe that a car built at that time would still be in running condition. The fact is, though, that there are always about three hundred cars in the London to Brighton Run and most of them chug along quite happily. The oldest entry in recent years has been a lovely old 1893 Benz.

Horses vs.
Horseless Carriages

The first motoring event between London and Brighton took place on November 14, 1896. The Light Road Locomotives Act had just been passed. The race was held to celebrate the motorists' victory. In spite of shouts of protest from many quarters, the speed limit had been raised to the breathtaking speed of 12 miles (19 km) per hour.

But that wasn't all. The Act also stated that it was no longer necessary for a man carrying a red flag to precede each car, warning pedestrians of the approaching danger. "Emancipation has come to British drivers at last," Harry Lawson, president of the Motor Car Club, declared jubilantly. He then tore a red flag to tatters and tossed the pieces into the air.

Forty-one cars were lined up and ready to roll on the morning of the race. The two American entries were both Duryea motor wagons. Five of the British entries were one-and-a-half-horsepower Arnold dogcarts entered by Andrew Arnold himself. The Germans had sent over a couple of Daimlers. France, the world's leading car producer at that time, shipped fourteen cars and three De Dion tricycles to London. There were also four delivery vans entered in the race.

One of the entries really had no business being there at all. It wasn't a car or a van or a tricycle. It wasn't even a horseless carriage. It was, in fact, a carriage drawn by four horses. The owner was a man named Hilbert Walter and Walter hated cars with a passion. He was going to prove to everyone that horses were faster and more reliable than cars.

The president of the Motor Car Club didn't like Walter's attitude even a little bit. He curtly told the man to take his horses and get lost. But Walter was a man with a mind of his

Over: *a double-decker bus follows hard on the tail of an entry in a London to Brighton Vintage Car Run.*

own. The road to Brighton was a public road, he told the president. It had been built for horses and carriages and not for cars. He was going to Brighton in his carriage and not even the Queen of England could stop him.

It was exactly ten-thirty when the official starter fired his pistol. Twenty-seven vehicles and a carriage drawn by four horses immediately went racing off toward Brighton. The other fourteen vehicles got off to a less dramatic start. They couldn't get going under their own power, so they had to holler for help. After that, though, they rolled along rather nicely until further problems developed.

The major problems, however, developed in Brighton. Just three hours after the start of the race, three British cars came chugging across the finish line. An official did some quick figuring, then announced that the drivers had moved at an average speed of 15 miles (24 km) an hour.

This really wasn't good news at all. The speed limit was still 12 miles (19 km) an hour in Britain and the law also applied to car races. There were no exceptions. Fortunately, luck was on the side of the three racing drivers. The official timekeeper's car had broken down while still inside the London city limits and there was no way to prove that the men had exceeded the speed limit.

Soon after the arrival of the first three cars in Brighton, some ugly gossip began to fly. Several people said that they had seen the cars arrive on the train from London. It was just over an hour from London to Brighton by train and the vehicles could travel very comfortably on a flatcar. A lady even reported seeing one of the men splashing his car with mud to give it a well-journeyed look.

While the officials were trying to decide what to do, Hilbert Walter came galloping into town. He freely admitted that he had changed horses five times along the way. Then he added that he had not seen a single motor car since leaving London.

Nobody really knows for sure, but it looks as though all the horseless carriages in the London to Brighton Race of 1896 were beaten by a carriage and four horses.

Top Speed—
20 Miles (32 km) an Hour

The last actual "race" between London and Brighton was run in 1930. It was won by a 1903 De Dietrich and the first prize was $200. Since that time, racing between the two cities has been discouraged. The British Motor Car Act of 1903 raised the speed limit to 20 miles (32 km) an hour. That was adopted as the top speed for the London to Brighton Vintage Car Run and that's what it still is today.

Speed is of no importance at all. Cars leave Hyde Park in London at eight in the morning. Anyone who reaches Brighton before four in the afternoon is considered a finisher and is awarded a plaque to prove it. The entire run is only 52 miles (84 km). Drivers who can maintain an average speed of 6.5 miles (10.5 km) an hour will be able to go home with a plaque. Vehicles are frequently passed by bicycles and joggers, but nobody really minds.

Not surprisingly, the Vintage Car Run often attracts some of the top racing aces. World champions such as Jackie Stewart, Stirling Moss, Jack Brabham, and a number of others have chugged cheerfully from London to Brighton at 20 miles (32 km) an hour. This, of course, is a far call from the breakneck speeds they have to maintain in other motoring events. Daytona and Indianapolis may be more demanding, but the Vintage Car Run is a lot more fun.

And that's what it's all about. People love a good time and the London to Brighton Run is fun for everyone. Even the two men who had to push their tricycle the last 7 miles (11 km) in the 1979 Run insisted that they had had a good time.

(13)
THE LONDON TO SYDNEY MARATHON

If you look at the globe in your classroom, you'll see that London, England is not too far from the top of the world. Sydney, on the continent of Australia, is pretty close to the bottom. In nice round figures, there are about 10,000 miles (16,000 km) of driving between London and Sydney.

Now 10,000 miles (16,000 km) is a very long drive. It seems even farther when you have to drive just as fast as you can every inch of the way. That was the object of the race, though. The first car to reach Sydney would win a $25,000 prize.

Rally officials who had gone over the route had some hair-raising stories to tell. Drivers had to average 1,000 miles (1,600 km) a day. The route was particularly tough in some sections of Asia and Australia. The road snaked through snow-capped mountains and sliced across dust-dry deserts. It was often little more than a rocky track. And the rocks, said the officials, came in three sizes: large, extra large, and enormous.

The people were also interesting. Customs and immigration officers in Asia could sometimes be terribly efficient. Everything had to be checked and double-checked. This could easily take an hour or more. Eager young policemen were known to arrest anyone exceeding the local speed limit. People in Pakistan and India often walked down the middle of the road and refused to move. Playful Turkish children amused themselves by throwing rocks at the windshields of approaching cars. Afghan bandits in the Khyber Pass, however, preferred rifles to rocks.

Drivers listened to these stories and looked at each other nervously. The London to Sydney Marathon, it appeared, ought to be lots and lots of fun.

The Fun Begins

The sun was shining on London's Crystal Palace Stadium on the morning of November 24, 1968. Ninety-eight cars were ready to start rolling off to Sydney. Teams from Britain, the Soviet Union, Belgium, France, Germany, Japan, Poland, Australia, and Finland were there. The lone American entry was a Rambler piloted by Syd Dickson of California.

A British team had the doubtful distinction of being the first to fall by the wayside. The driver flicked a cigarette butt out the window while cruising merrily along at 70 miles (113 km) an hour. Unfortunately, the butt blew straight back into the car and hit him smack in the eye. There was a howl of pain, then cries of rage from the two team members as the car shot off the road and into the kitchen of a farmhouse.

Those who wrecked their cars in Turkey and other parts of Asia had more serious problems. They were a long way from anywhere and it was a lot harder to holler for help. In some cases, in fact, it was just about impossible. One of the German entries is a good example of this.

The big Mercedes missed a curve in Pakistan's Khyber Pass and went rolling helplessly down a cliffside. It came to rest upside down on the bank of an icy-blue mountain stream. None of the Germans was badly hurt, but all three of them wished very much that they were back home in Germany.

Over: a Russian entry in the London to Sydney Marathon makes its way through a village in the Khyber Pass.

Although the Germans were not happy, they were not in the least lonely. Robed tribesmen wearing turbans appeared out of nowhere. Most of them carried rifles and most of them sported fierce mustaches. Some came with their camels, others with their goats, and a few even brought their families. They had never seen Germans or an upside-down Mercedes before.

The Germans were excited, too, but for an entirely different reason. It was getting late. The Khyber Pass was crawling with bandits and was no place for a foreigner to be after dark. They would have to get out of there—and fast!

But where could they go? And how would they get there? They were somewhere in the wilds between Rawalpindi, Pakistan and Kabul, Afghanistan. Walking was out of the question and there was no chance at all of getting the Mercedes back on its wheels. Renting a camel and heading for civilization didn't seem to be the answer, either.

A cloud of dust boiled up in the distance while the Germans were trying to decide what to do. Seconds later, a battered Moskvitch skidded to a halt beside them. The window was rolled down and three Russians peered out. Their car had been sideswiped by a truck in Afghanistan, but they were still in the rally.

The long trip to Rawalpindi was not a pleasant one. The Moskvitch was a small car and the three Russians and three Germans were all big men. To make things even worse, the car was packed tightly with luggage, foodstuffs, tools, and spare parts.

Welcome to Bombay

Seven days after leaving London, seventy-two cars rolled into Bombay, India. Twenty-six others had come to grief in various places along the 7,000-mile (11,200 km) route. A few had fallen out because of mechanical problems, but most had been involved in rather spectacular crashes.

Those who reached Bombay had also had their moments of drama. Syd Dickson, the American entry, drove straight through a Turkish house. A British team missed a corner in Iran, shot down a hillside at terrifying speed, hit the road again, and kept on going. Another British team managed to sail off a bridge and into the Indus River. Several cars had been stoned by gangs of young toughs in Pakistan. The three Australian women sponsored by the Sydney *Daily Telegraph* insisted that they had been ambushed by bandits in the Khyber Pass.

Everyone's favorite story was told by an English team from Manchester. An Indian policeman had stopped them and ordered them in no uncertain terms to obey the local speed limits. If they didn't observe the laws, he told them, they would find themselves in deep trouble. Having given them a stern lecture, the policeman sent them on their way. Unfortunately, he neglected to step out of the way and the driver drove over his foot.

With Sydney Almost in Sight

It was Friday the thirteenth of December when the seventy-two cars were unloaded in Perth, Australia. The teams had had a good rest on board ship and they were ready to roll. Sydney was somewhat over 3,000 miles (4,800 km) to the east. That meant a long drive over terrible roads, but it had to be done in three days.

The Australian teams boasted proudly that their roads were even worse than those in Turkey and Afghanistan. It was dust all the way, they said, and they were right. It was also rocks and potholes. One particularly large pothole put three cars out of the running.

The great emptiness of the Australian Outback staggered the European entries. There were thousands of square miles of absolutely nothing. Tiny collections of nondescript shacks bore such strange-sounding names as Wagga Wagga, Tooka Toota, and Beena Mooka. There was also a dried up riverbed called the Poopa Singga.

As the cars got deeper and deeper into Australia, one thing became very clear: Lucien Bianchi, a Belgian, was the man to beat. He had been driving magnificently all the way. His odd-looking Citroen actually seemed to like the awful roads and he literally flew over them.

Bianchi was a very happy man. His car may have looked odd, but it had behaved beautifully. He had pounded it along at top speed for over 10,000 miles (16,000 km) and it had never let him down.

The roads got better as Sydney got closer. Bianchi was well in the lead. There was no longer any reason to hurry. If nothing unforeseen happened, the $25,000 prize would soon be in his pocket.

But something unforeseen did happen. Less than 50 miles (80 km) from Sydney, an old rattletrap of a car came racing down the highway. It was weaving crazily from one side of the road to the other. Bianchi took every avoiding action possible, but the car smashed into him head-on and burst into flame. Rescue teams had to cut the Belgian out of his wrecked Citroen with cutting torches.

(14)
BRITAIN'S *WILD* AND WOOLY WORLD CUP RALLY

It was the morning of April 19, 1970. Ninety-six cars were lined up in London's huge Wembley Stadium. They were all ready to roll. Nobody, though, was more ready to roll than Bobby Buchanan. Lucky Bobby had won the Number One position. He was to be the first to leave Wembley Stadium and he was absolutely determined to be the first to reach Mexico City.

The official starter swung his flag at exactly ten-thirty in the morning. The crowd roared as Bobby went roaring down the ramp. He roared for no more than 25 yards (23 m) before his engine sputtered, snorted, wheezed, and then died.

One car after the other rolled away on the first leg of the World Cup Rally. Nearly everyone shouted something at Bobby as he drove past. An Australian driver, however, laughed so hard at poor Bobby that he drove into a cement pillar and smashed a headlight.

It took nearly half an hour to get the car running properly. They had lost a lot of time and Bobby tried his best to make up at least a few precious minutes. When he heard the scream of a police siren behind him, he realized sadly that he had been trying just a little bit too hard.

The policeman was both firm and fair. He listened sympathetically while Bobby explained that he was in the World Cup Rally and was on his way to Mexico City. That was all very interesting and exciting, smiled the policeman, but it didn't give him the right to race through the streets of London. He then wrote out a ticket for speeding and handed it to Bobby.

Bobby Buchanan managed a weak little smile as he rolled slowly out into the line of traffic. "Thank goodness there's only another 16,238 miles (26,143 km) to go," he said to his teammates.

A Rally to Rave About

The World Cup Rally was dreamed up by the people at the London *Daily Mirror*. The *Mirror* likes wild stories and thought that a race from London to Mexico City would be very wild indeed. They got their story and it was wild enough to suit just about everyone.

The drivers were not going to race directly to Mexico City, of course. That would be much too easy. The organizers wanted the rally to be as tough as possible, so they planned a course that was particularly difficult. Even the most experienced drivers turned a bit pale when they saw the route map.

After leaving London, the cars would continue east as far as Bulgaria. They would then swing west and head for Lisbon, Portugal. From Lisbon, they would be shipped across the Atlantic to Rio de Janeiro in Brazil.

Everyone believed that South America would be the great proving ground. There would be time to rest in Rio, but then the real battle would begin. The route went south from Rio to the pampas of Argentina before crossing over to Chile on the Pacific Coast. It then followed the backbone of the skyscraping Andes Mountains for practically the entire length of the South American continent. Anyone still in the rally at that point would only have Panama, the five Central American republics, and Mexico left to go.

All told, the route went through twenty-five countries. It covered an estimated 16,241 miles (26,148 km). That would be a terribly long drive under perfect conditions, but everyone knew that conditions would be very far from perfect. In fact, they would be terrible for much of the way. Casualty rates were expected to be very high. Then, of course, there were those who declared that no one would make it all the way to Mexico City.

In spite of the gloomy predictions, response to the rally was tremendous. Ninety-six cars from seventeen different countries made up the official list of entries, including women from all over the world.

There were also three paupers and a prince in the rally. The paupers were three Mexican students in a badly beat-up Volkswagen Beetle. They were doing quite well until they ran out of money in Spain. The prince was His Royal Highness Prince Michael of Kent. He was also doing quite well until he ran out of road in Uruguay and smashed his car.

Most of the cars entered looked very much like the cars you see on the road every day. There were a few, though, that looked rather out-of-place in the lineup. One was the Volkswagen Beetle and another was a Beach Buggy that appeared to be in very poor condition.

Perhaps the most unlikely entries were two stately Rolls Royces. Both were piloted by British businessmen. The crews were wearing tuxedos, bowler hats, and monocles when they rolled majestically out of Wembley Stadium. A great chorus of cheers rolled out with them.

An Earthquake and a Flying Finn

The European section of the route turned out to be tougher than anyone had expected. It was springtime and the melting snow meant floods and washouts. Landslides were common in the Alps, Pyrenees, and Balkans.

A dozen or so cars were tearing along a horribly rutted road in Yugoslavia when strange things began to happen: Frightened people came running out of their houses. Dogs howled. Huge rocks came bounding down the mountainside. Trees swayed, but there was no wind to sway them.

The drivers raced cheerfully on. They were bouncing around so much that they didn't even notice the earthquake. There was nothing they could have done about it anyway, of course. They were tearing along a narrow mountain road. All they could do was keep on going and hope for the best.

A British team kept on going even when they no longer had a road under them. The earthquake had triggered a landslide which had carried a part of the road down the mountainside. The car came ripping around a corner and suddenly found itself sailing through space. The area was heavily forested and the car went crashing down among the treetops. It wasn't a gentle descent by any means, but the trees did cushion the impact. The car crunched its way down through the branches until it came to rest on the floor of the forest. Except for a bad scare and a big shaking up, the crew was unhurt. Their car, though, had to stay where it landed.

Hannu Mikkola, now known as The Flying Finn, also did a bit of sailing in Yugoslavia. The rally had screeched to a halt on the bank of a river near the Bulgarian border. There was a rickety wooden bridge across the river, but it was missing a number of planks from the center.

The scene was one of utter confusion. Several men were running along the bank trying to find enough timber to patch the gap in the bridge. Still others were studying their maps in the hope of finding another route.

The Finn studied the gap for a minute or two, then turned to Gunnar Palm, his Swedish codriver. "You know," he said thoughtfully, "I believe I can jump that."

Palm's eyes almost jumped out of his head. "You believe that you can *what* that?" he wanted to know.

"Come on," said Mikkola. "Let's give it a try."

The Swede wasn't happy. He didn't like this sort of thing at all. The narrow, rickety bridge didn't even have a guard rail. If anything went wrong, they'd most likely be out of the rally. Palm wanted to close his eyes, but he was afraid to.

Mikkola drove back up the road for 100 yards (91 m) or so before turning around. Without saying a word, he slammed the car into gear and took off. The speedometer was on 75 (121) when the front wheels touched the first planks. The Finn stamped down harder on the gas and the heavy car sailed smoothly across the gap. "We made it!" Mikkola yelled triumphantly. "We made it!"

Not everyone, though, had The Flying Finn's kind of luck. Twenty-five cars failed to complete the European Section of the World Cup Rally. The remaining seventy-one were to be shipped across the Atlantic for the long, hard drive from Rio de Janeiro to Mexico City.

And there were still those who said that none of the cars would ever get there.

(15)
THE RALLY GETS
WILDER AND WOOLIER

The crews flew to Brazil and had twelve days to relax in Rio while waiting for their cars to arrive by sea. Nineteen of the seventy-one cars which later left Rio failed to make it to Montevideo. His Royal Highness Prince Michael of Kent was one of the casualties. There was a story going around that the prince was going to be kidnapped by bandits in Uruguay. This might possibly have been the reason for the accident. The prince might have been watching out for bandits instead of watching the road.

Rally drivers don't frighten easily, but the traffic in Buenos Aires terrified them. They had never seen anything like it. Everyone drove like a madman. There were almost no traffic lights and drivers charged one another at breakneck speed. The accident rate was beyond belief.

Knowing that the foreigners might have some problems, the police arranged to escort them out of the city. It was a drive none of them will ever forget. The police took off in a fierce burst of speed with sirens screaming. By the time they reached the outskirts of the city, three police vehicles and two rally cars had been involved in traffic accidents. Both of the rally cars, however, were able to continue on their way.

To everyone's surprise, only nine cars failed to finish the stretch between Buenos Aires in Argentina and Santiago in Chile. Crossing the South American continent had not been quite as tough as expected. The truly tough part was still in front of them. Those who had surveyed the route gave little shudders when they described the horrors of racing through Bolivia and Peru.

The Bolivian *altiplano* is a barren plain 12,000 feet (3,668 m) above sea level. Although not many tourists visit the region, there are some interesting things to see. Rally drivers saw splendid snowcapped peaks, llamas, alpacas, and Indians who are direct descendents of the mighty Incas. They also saw a horse in the roof rack of a car. Red Redgrave had clobbered the poor animal while zipping along at top speed. The horse had been hit with such force that it literally sailed right onto the roof. Now Redgrave and his two teammates were trying to get it off.

David Smith and his crew also had an interesting experience in Bolivia. They were driving through a village when two policemen suddenly appeared in the road and waved their rifles at them. Smith immediately shot down a side street. Unfortunately, it turned out to be a dead end and he had to back up straight toward the policemen.

The policemen were furious. One fired several shots into the air to show the foreigners that they meant business. The other whipped out his pistol and aimed it at the tip of Smith's nose. Both of the officers were shouting nonstop in Spanish.

Smith was afraid that his nose might be blown off at any minute. He didn't understand a word that was being said. He realized, though, that the policemen wanted something, so he began handing them things. He handed them a box of dried figs, a thermos of black coffee, his passport and other personal papers, a pack of English cigarettes, and a photograph of his wife and children.

Nothing could have pleased the policemen more. They "oh-d" and "ah-d" over the photograph and beamed a big smile at each page in Smith's passport. The cigarettes and figs delighted them and they made little contented sounds while slurping their coffee.

A French crew wasn't that lucky. Peruvian police arrested them in Ayacucho and they were locked up in the local jail for five days. That was in May, 1970 and the men still don't know today why they were arrested.

It was also in Peru that a team from Scotland found itself in big trouble. The driver drove through a chain stretched across the road at an Army checkpoint. Although the driver repaired the chain and paid a fine, the soldier on duty wanted to shoot him. It took the worried Scotsman a full five minutes and a carton of cigarettes to talk the soldier out of it.

The biggest problem of all in Bolivia and Peru was the road itself. It was in terrible condition. Conditions in general were terrible. Cars had to cross the Ticlio Pass at an elevation of 15,870 feet (4,825 m) and nearly everyone suffered severely from altitude sickness.

Thirty battered cars came limping into Lima, the capital of Peru. The casualty rate now stood at a staggering sixty-six. Drivers felt, though, that the toughest part of the rally was behind them. They had driven 12,000 miles (19,300 km) and Mexico City was now a mere 4,000 miles (6,400 km) away.

At Buenaventura in Colombia, cars and crews were loaded onto an Italian steamer. As soon as the ship docked in Panama, the drivers headed for their hotels. They all wanted to get a good night's sleep. Their next stop was Mexico City and they had to be up early.

Hans Katz, a German entry, arrived at the docks at sunrise. He soon suspected that everything was not as it should be. The rally cars had been parked in a nice, neat line, but his Mercedes was nowhere in the lineup.

An official of the Italian steamship company soon located the missing Mercedes. Somebody had made a mistake. For some unknown reason, the German's car had not been off-loaded in Panama. It was now on its way across the Atlantic to Italy.

Everyone felt sorry for the German, but nothing could be done. His luck had simply run out. Drivers shook their heads in sympathy as they drove past Hans Katz. The German was stamping furiously along the dock and roaring with anger. The other drivers knew that they would have felt the same way if the same thing had happened to them.

There was some more sympathetic shaking of heads when Claudine Trautmann smashed her car in southern Mexico. It was the second cruel blow that the Trautmann family had suffered in the World Cup Rally. René, Claudine's husband, had been leading the field until he crashed in Uruguay. At the time of her accident, Claudine was leading the women. She had bravely battled along for 15,000 punishing miles (24,000 km), but the Ladies Prize went to Rosemarie Smith.

Twenty-three cars rolled proudly into Mexico City. They were led by Hannu Mikkola, The Flying Finn. A total of seventy-three cars had failed to finish.

It had been a long, hard haul, but some drivers were already talking about the next World Cup Rally. An Australian suggested a race from the North Pole to the South Pole and some liked the idea.

One even said that it sounded like fun.

(16)
THE EAST AFRICAN SAFARI

Drivers just don't know what to think about the Safari. It has been called the meanest and most miserable car contest imaginable. It has also been called the most exciting motoring event of the year.

"For my money, the Safari is the toughest and best road rally in the world," says professional rally driver Patricia Moss-Carlsson.

"The Safari stinks, but I love it," says her brother Stirling Moss, former world racing champion.

Moss has good reason to say that the Safari stinks. It is one race that he simply cannot win. He comes back to East Africa year after year and the story is always the same: Something goes wrong and he fails to finish.

He did, however, come very close on one occasion. He was less than 100 miles (160 km) from the finishing line in Nairobi when he piled head-on into a herd of wildebeests. "I was a bit disappointed," he told a reporter.

Not a single professional rally driver has ever won the Safari. Many of the very best have tried, but their tries just weren't good enough. The best example by far is Erik Carlsson. The Magnificent Swede, as he is affectionately called in East Africa, has had a grand total of ten tries. Although Carlsson has won every other major rally in the world, the Safari beats him every time.

The names of men who win the Safari are unknown outside of East Africa. These men probably wouldn't put on much of a show at Indianapolis, Daytona Beach, or Monaco. On their home ground, however, they're almost impossible to beat.

There's a perfectly good reason for this, of course: Driving in East Africa is not like driving anywhere else on earth. The mud there is muddier, the rocks are rockier, and the dust is dustier. The mountain roads seem to be more mountainous and even the miles seem to be more than 5,280 feet (1,609 m).

And then there are the animals. Great concentrations of game are a common sight on the East African plains. It's fun to watch them, but they can be a menace. They cross the road whenever they please, often causing problems for many motorists.

Safari drivers have hit everything from little Thomson's gazelles to huge, hulking hippos. Rhinos, buffaloes, and elephants have challenged the Safari's right to use the road. A giraffe once stuck its foot through the windshield of a competitor's car. Mike Doughty and his partner told about repairing their radiator while a pride of twelve lions sat watching them. An official in the 1980 event hit a buck less than twenty minutes out of Nairobi.

A Rough and Rugged Rally Is Born

It all began in 1953, when a group of Nairobi businessmen decided that a road rally would be good fun. It would also answer some questions. The results would let people know which cars stood up best to the horrible pounding that vehicles take in that part of the world.

The organizers had a great time. Grinning gleefully, they mapped out a 2,000-mile (3,200 km) route of rough roads twisting through Kenya, Tanzania, and Uganda. The course crossed and recrossed the equator. It skirted the snow-capped peaks of Kilimanjaro and Mount Kenya, then plunged down to the palm-lined beaches of the Indian Ocean. To make things more interesting, the rally was scheduled for the Easter weekend. This was the time of the year when tropical storms turned roads into rivers of red mud.

Fifty-seven cars raced off from Nairobi, Kenya on the morning of Good Friday. Although mud and wild animals exacted a heavy toll, sixteen cars managed to finish within the time limits. By the following evening, all the cars except a little Morris Minor had come limping in.

"What do you suppose could have happened?" asked a worried official.

"I don't know," replied another, then added, "Maybe something ate it."

Nothing had, though. A light plane spotted it in a huge mud hole the next day.

The first East African Safari was such a great success that the organizers decided to make it an annual event. Some of the drivers, however, had a complaint: They said that the rally wasn't tough enough. The organizers agreed at once and cheerfully lengthened the route to a bone-rattling 3,300 miles (5,300 km).

(17)
THE SAFARI ENTERS THE BIG TIME

The challenge of the Safari fired the imagination of the motoring world. Professional rally drivers began appearing in Nairobi and the friendly East Africans gave them a warm welcome. They were proud of the fact that their little homegrown rally was becoming an international competition.

It wasn't long before the little homegrown rally became a motoring epic. Fortunately, the big attraction in this case was not money. Winning the Safari would not make the winner a rich man. Not by any means. Most drivers signed up for the Safari because it was wildly exciting and lots of fun.

Then, too, it was also a terrific challenge. The fact that the rally was always won by a local amateur had become something of a joke. The professionals simply could not finish first. Factories sent their best cars and drivers to Nairobi, but it didn't do any good. Some East African farmboy was always the first one home.

Actually, though, an overseas driver could probably have won the 1979 event if he hadn't been such a nice guy. Shekhar Mehta and Mike Doughty of Kenya were in the lead when they got stuck in the mud. Two Finnish drivers helped them out, then went racing off. Mehta and Doughty raced after them and beat the Finns to Nairobi. For the twenty-sixth consecutive time, local amateurs walked away with the prize money.

It's an unwritten law in East Africa that a driver must give anyone in trouble a helping hand. This applies to the rally drivers as well. Eric Cecil, one of the Safari's founders, says, "It's part of the game to stop and help the other fellow with a push or a tow or a spare part when you know that in doing so it's costing you precious time."

Nearly everyone in East Africa is a Safari fan and will do just about anything to help the drivers. A farmer in Nanyuki gave Bill Parkinson the radiator from his car. Bill had smashed his in a collision with a warthog and needed a replacement. The farmer couldn't go anywhere without a radiator, of course, but he didn't seem to mind that at all. He was happy to help someone in the Safari.

A Safari fan also saved the day for Vic Preston and D. P. Marwaha. They broke an axle near Kisumu very early one morning. There was only one other car like theirs in the town, they were told, and it belonged to a certain young woman.

The sun was not yet up when Preston knocked on the woman's door. "What do you want?" a sleepy voice called from inside.

"We want to borrow your rear axle," Preston called back.

The door was jerked open and the woman glared angrily at the bearded, haggard men. "You want to borrow my rear *what?*" she demanded.

"Well, we're in the Safari, you see," Preston explained. His face was very red and he was talking very fast. "We broke our rear axle and we'd like to borrow yours."

"Oh, you're in the Safari!" the woman exclaimed, her anger forgotten. "That's different. Take anything you want."

"Thanks so much," Preston told her. "Just your rear axle will be fine."

The woman was delighted when Preston phoned the next day. Her rear axle, he happily told her, had been the first rear axle to cross the finish line in Nairobi.

Once again, the Safari had been won by a couple of the local boys.

Local Boys Always
Make Good—So Far

Although the Safari had become big business by the 1970s, both the organizers and the drivers wanted as few changes as possible. It wrecked cars and frayed nerves, but it was also good fun. There was not another rally like it anywhere in the world.

Overseas drivers who came to Nairobi always enjoyed themselves greatly. The Safari was a challenge that they just couldn't resist. They knew, though, that the odds were against them.

The local boys continued to win year after year. Joginder Singh, a name unknown outside of East Africa, won the Safari three times. He most likely would have had a fourth win if he hadn't banged into a buffalo. That gave local boys Bert Shankland and Chris Rothwell their first victory. It was also the first time that not a single one of the overseas drivers managed to finish.

Nobody can seriously doubt the fact that the Safari will someday be won by a professional rally driver. The manufacturers will see to that. They're willing to spend piles of money in East Africa. If their car wins, it will mean millions of dollars worth of publicity. People feel that a car tough enough to survive the Safari ought to be tough enough to survive just about anything.

The Safari is still a lot of fun. The roads are still horrible and someone is always banging into a beast of some kind. Anything can go wrong and usually does. Rain may fall for hours and hours. Mechanical breakdowns occur constantly. Bridges have to be rebuilt and suspensions repaired. No matter how grim things get, though, the drivers keep on smiling. Or at least they try to.

Nothing ever stays exactly the same. This, of course, is also true of the Safari. There have been many changes since Good Friday 1953. A driver who ran into trouble then got himself out of it as best he could. Drivers today are often able to radio for help when they run into trouble.

When Professionals
Lose to Amateurs

The weeks before Easter are a time of frenzied activity in Nairobi. Visitors arriving at the Jomo Kenyatta International Airport probably think that a huge military operation is underway. Rally cars, service cars, and tons of supplies are being unloaded from huge cargo planes. Men with worried looks on their faces are running around all over the place.

Nothing is left to chance. Manufacturers make very sure that the rally drivers have everything they could possibly need. A great deal of money is involved and a win in the Safari is very important to them. East African drivers, however, find the whole thing very amusing. They've been driving these roads for years carrying nothing but a few spares, a couple of tools, and a cooler full of beer. It's hard for them not to smile at all the elaborate preparations.

And the preparations are truly elaborate. The German firm of Mercedes-Benz, for example, entered six cars in 1979. Twelve service cars and a mountain of supplies were sent to Nairobi to care for the needs of the six entries. A command plane, a supply plane, and a helicopter were also a part of the Mercedes-Benz scene.

Fiat of Italy spent millions of dollars on its four rally cars. The sixteen drivers who flew to Nairobi were accompanied by twenty mechanics, three team managers, a team doctor, and countless crates of spares. A helicopter and a supply plane arrived the next day.

The saddest story of the 1979 Safari concerns the French team of Peugeot. Eighteen service cars and two airplanes were on hand to support the four entries. Technicians were everywhere. The story of the French team is short as well as sad. Two of the four cars crashed the first day and another went out with mechanical troubles. The fourth and last car fell by the wayside on the second day. It was all over for the unlucky French.

Well, not quite over. Peugeot had been so sure of winning that they had sent cases and cases of champagne to Nairobi. Unfortunately, there was no victory to celebrate. There was no sense in taking the champagne back to Paris, of course, so the unhappy Frenchmen used it to drown their sorrows.

It is not known if the French team saved any of their victory champagne for Shekhar Mehta and Mike Doughty, the two Kenyans who won the 1979 Safari. If they didn't, they can hardly be blamed. Neither Mehta nor Doughty are professional rally drivers.

They only sign up for the Safari because it's lots and lots of fun.

(18)
MEN WHO RACE AGAINST THE CLOCK

The man who had the world's first car wanted to know how fast it would go. That bit of information can't be found in any book on racing, but it's almost certain to be true. Why? Because men have always been fascinated by speed. That was true one hundred years ago and it's true today. It will also be true one hundred years from now.

In 1875, the state of Wisconsin offered a large cash prize to anyone who could come up with "a cheap and satisfactory substitute for the horse." A man by the name of Joshua Shomer believed that he had just the thing. He was building a vehicle he called the Oshkosh Steamer. When it was completed, he would show the state of Wisconsin what it could do.

Early on the morning of July 16, 1878, Shomer rolled out of Green Bay, Wisconsin at top speed. The next day, he puffed into Madison and parked his Oshkosh Steamer in front of the Wisconsin state capitol. He had driven 231 miles (372 km) in just thirty-three hours and twenty-seven minutes. In round figures, he had averaged 7 miles (11 km) an hour.

"That," said an excited businessman, aiming a finger at Shomer's car, "is the transportation of the future."

A friend agreed. "It's at least twice as fast as walking," he said, obviously impressed by the Steamer's speed.

The Age of Speed Begins
It must have occurred to most people that cars even faster than Joshua Shomer's Oshkosh Steamer would soon be on the

road. It's true that 7 miles (11 km) an hour was a pretty fair clip, but Americans have always wanted to go faster and faster. We are people in a hurry and speed is important to us.

The Age of Speed came sooner than expected. It was ushered in by our old friend Red Devil Jenatzy on April 29, 1899. Jenatzy was driving an electric car that he had built himself. On a track outside of Paris, the Belgian hit 66 miles (106 km) an hour. This was more than one mile (1.6 km) a minute and made Red Devil the fastest man in the world.

A mile a minute! It was almost beyond belief. Such speed simply boggled the mind. People talked of little else for days and days. Red Devil Jenatzy's name was on everyone's lips. His face became almost as familiar to people as the face of President William McKinley. (The President of the United States, of course, did not have flaming red hair and a bushy red beard.)

Henry Ford, a name known to all of us, was the next one to make racing history. On January 12, 1904, he was clocked at 91 miles (146 km) an hour. This was more than 1½ miles (2.4 km) a minute. A new world record had been set and America had a racing hero.

Heroes come and heroes go. In Henry Ford's case, he went very fast. Just fifteen days after setting a new world record, it was broken by William K. Vanderbilt. Unfortunately, the world's richest man didn't hang onto the record for very long, either. It was broken a few months later when a Frenchman named Louis Rigolly broke the 100-miles (160 km)-an-hour mark. Victor Hemery, also a Frenchman, soon broke Rigolly's record by hitting 2 miles (3.2 km) a minute at Daytona Beach.

Over: *two of America's earliest racing heroes were Barney Oldfield and Henry Ford (standing). Oldfield drove Ford's famous 999 to several victories in 1903.*

The Stanley Steamers
Retire from Racing

There was a great flurry of racing on the Florida beaches in the early years of the twentieth century. Men like Louis Chevrolet and Henry Ford were racing cars they had built themselves. Barney Oldfield was racing any car he could get his hands on. The Stanley twins were also in Florida, but Fred Marriott was doing the driving.

Nobody seems to know exactly why, but the racing people treated the Stanley twins very badly. Ford and Chevrolet heaped scorn on the funny-looking little steamers. Oldfield expressed doubt about Marriott's ability to race a car. Officials on several occasions "forgot" to record Marriott's speed. On another occasion, Marriott's time to race was moved up from nine in the morning to seven in the morning. The officials, however, "forgot" to tell him.

In spite of all the hanky-panky, Marriott set a new world record of 128 miles (206 km) an hour. A few days later, he hit a rough bit of beach while moving at an estimated speed of 150 miles (241 km) an hour. The car sailed through the air for 100 feet (30 m) before landing on its nose. Marriott was hurled into the surf. The car was demolished and Stanley Steamers were never raced again. "We do not believe in risking a man's life solely for the sake of speed," said the Stanley twins.

Faster and Still Faster

A most peculiar sort of unofficial speed record was set at Ormond Beach, Florida in 1922. It was set by Sig Haugdahl in a Wisconsin Special. Haugdahl stunned spectators and officials by moving at 180 miles (290 km) an hour, which is exactly 3 miles (4.8 km) a minute. The officials and spectators were even more stunned when Haugdahl swung away from the beach and headed home.

The weird behavior has never been explained. The rules stated clearly that a driver had to race over a measured mile in *both* directions. It was the average speed of the two runs that counted. Haugdahl knew that perfectly well. He also knew that he stood an excellent chance of setting a new world record.

Five years passed before a driver beat Haugdahl's unofficial record. That driver was Henry Segrave. The soft-spoken, smiling Englishman broke the 200-miles (320 km)-an-hour barrier at Daytona Beach in 1927.

The 300-miles (480 km)-an-hour barrier also fell to a citizen of Great Britain. On September 3, 1935, Malcolm Campbell became the fastest driver in the world for the ninth time. He broke the barrier in his Bluebird racing car at the Bonneville Salt Flats in Utah. Campbell, incidentally, is the only man who has held both the world's land and water speed records at the same time.

The next really big speed hurdle was, of course, the 400-miles (640 km)-an-hour barrier. Twenty-eight years went by before someone reached that speed on land. Unfortunately, the record was not recognized. Craig Breedlove, the handsome young driver, was told by officials that his car was not really a car.

Breedlove was understandably confused. "Well, if it's not a car, what is it?" he wanted to know.

Now it was the officials' turn to be confused. "It's more like . . . a motorcycle," they declared hesitantly.

But what a motorcycle! It looked like a jet fighter without wings. It was powered by a jet engine and weighed over three tons. There was one thing missing, however, and that was the fourth wheel. Breedlove's machine had only three wheels and therefore was not considered a car.

It was not until 1964 that the 400-miles (640 km)-an-hour barrier was broken. The driver who broke it was a citizen of Great Britain. His name was Donald Campbell. Just twenty-nine years earlier, Donald's famous father, Malcolm Campbell, had broken the 300-miles (480 km)-an-hour barrier.

Over: *Craig Breedlove was the first man to drive a car at 600 miles (960 km) an hour.*

This pair of events must surely rank as one of the most remarkable coincidences in the history of car racing.

After Donald Campbell's record-breaking run in 1964, things began to happen fast. The 500-miles (800 km)-an-hour barrier fell to Art Arfons and his "Green Monster" in 1965. Just a year later, Craig Breedlove drove his "Spirit of America" past the 600-miles (960 km)-an-hour mark. Racing officials had decided that Breedlove's motorcycle was a car after all. The young racer showed his appreciation by setting a new world record.

What Makes 'em Go So Fast?

Just a little more than one hundred years ago, 7 miles (11 km) an hour was thought to be a pretty fair rate of speed for a horseless carriage. In 1979, just a little over a century later, a horseless carriage moved nearly 106 times faster than that.

Way back in 1903, the electric car was the fastest thing on the road. The fastest and best ones were manufactured by the Baker Motor Vehicle Company. Walter Baker even built an electric racing car which he called the "Baker Torpedo." It was powered by twelve storage batteries and it went like a bomb. Unfortunately, the electric cars manufactured by the Baker Motor Vehicle Company had one serious shortcoming: After a mile or so, the batteries went dead.

For a time, steam-powered cars were the fastest things on wheels. Unlike other cars of the period, they were clean and quiet. They also seemed to have almost unlimited power. Sadly, though, the steam cars also had a serious shortcoming: They kept running out of steam.

The overwhelming majority of cars seen on roads and racetracks today are powered by gasoline. Some have their motors in front; others have them in the back. Some have four cylinders; many racing models have as many as twelve. Some have front-wheel drive; others have rear- or four-wheel drive. Although the horsepower, appearance, and many other things may vary immensely, nearly all cars have one thing in common: Nearly all of them have internal combustion engines.

This, of course, is not true in the few cases where men have raced their cars at speeds of more than 500 miles (800 km) an hour. Both Craig Breedlove and Art Arfons drove cars powered by jet airplane engines. Gary Gabelich's car, "The Blue Flame," was powered by a rocket engine burning liquified natural gas and hydrogen peroxide. The engine generated 16,000 pounds (7,200 kg) of thrust and Gabelich attained an average speed of 622 miles (1,001 km) an hour.

Naturally, cars like these are kept off the highways and country roads. They were built for speed and could never stay within the imposed 55-miles (88 km)-an-hour limit.

Smashing the Sound Barrier

You won't see anything like Stan Barrett's rocket car on the highway or parked in front of the supermarket. It's quite safe to say that because there's not another car in the whole world like Barrett's. His rocket car is 39 feet (12 m) long and only 20 inches (51 cm) wide. It has the power of fifty thousand horses. In just over one second, it can go from zero to 150 miles (240 km) an hour.

Although Stan Barrett was rather proud of his speed records, he wasn't entirely satisfied. He wanted to go still faster. In fact, he wanted to travel at the speed of sound. That meant that he would have to hit the incredible speed of 738 miles (1,188 km) an hour. Barrett wasn't at all worried. He was sure that he could do it.

Others weren't sure what to think. Some felt that the vehicle would simply fly apart at such a speed. The air was thicker on the ground than in the air and the pressure would be too great.

Over: in 1979 at Edwards Air Force Base in California, Stan Barrett's rocket car became the first land vehicle to break the sound barrier.

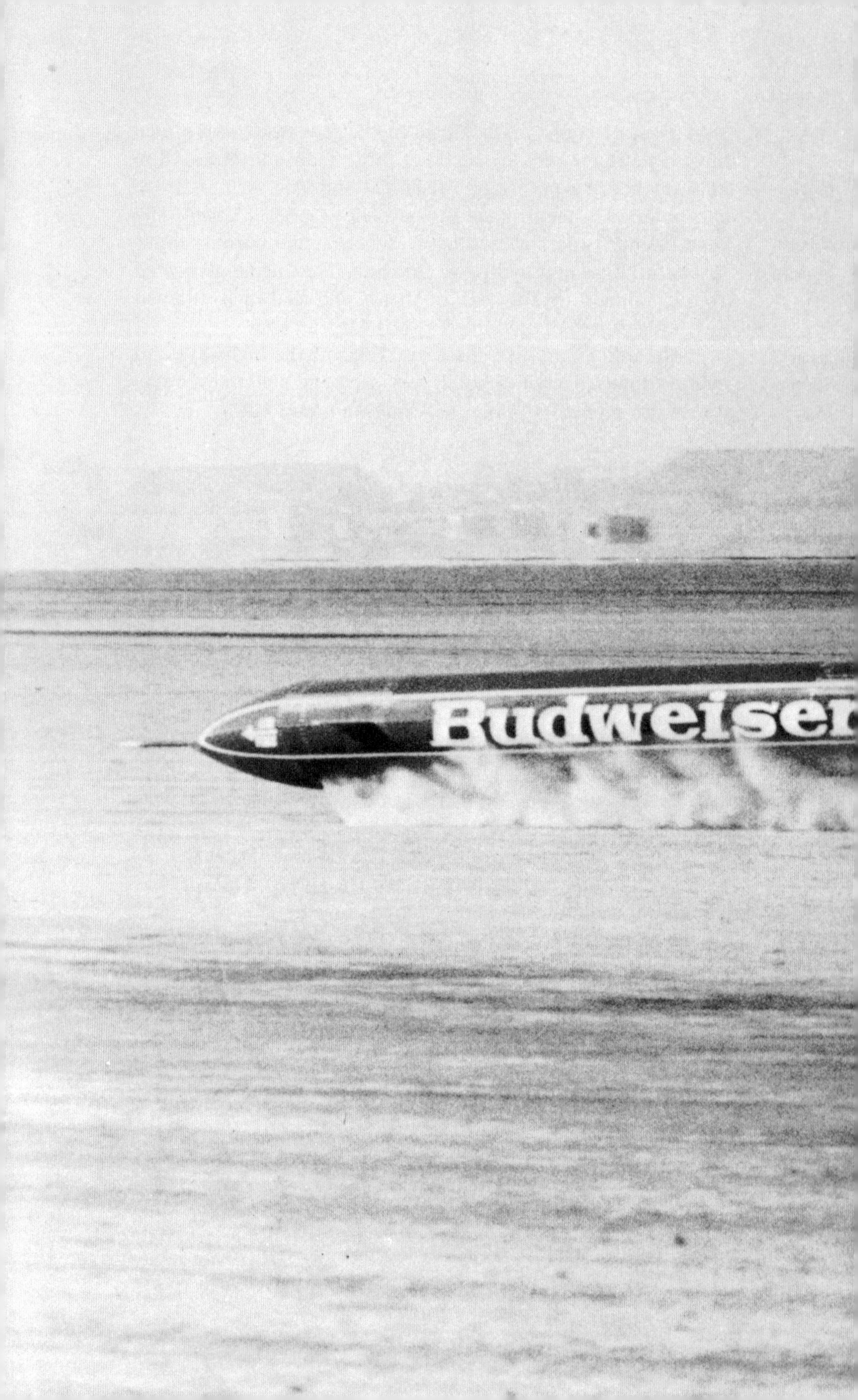
Budweiser

An aerodynamics engineer said the car might be lifted off the ground on its own pressure wave when it went through the sound barrier. It was easy, of course, to imagine what would happen when the car crashed back to earth. Barrett ignored the stories and went ahead with his plans. He is not the kind of man who scares easily.

December 17, 1979 was a beautiful day at the Edwards Air Force Base in California. Stan Barrett was smiling when he squeezed into the cockpit of his rocket car. The signal was given and he shot off across the dry lake bed. Just seconds later, officials and onlookers heard a dull boom. The sound barrier had been broken!

Instruments show that Barrett hit a top speed of 739.6 miles (1,190.5 km) an hour. His dream had come true and the performance of his rocket car delighted him. He's still not satisfied, though. Barrett would like to be the first man to hit 1,000 miles (1,600 km) an hour.

A Century of Speed

But Joshua Shomer and his Oshkosh Steamer should not be forgotten. Shomer was also delighted with the performance of his car. It had averaged 7 miles (11 km) an hour between Green Bay, Wisconsin and the state capitol building in Madison and that was a record for the time. That wasn't quite as fast as Stan Barrett's rocket car, it's true, but it wasn't bad at all for 1878.

After all, nobody had even heard of the sound barrier in those days, so Shomer wasn't even trying to break it.

FOR FURTHER READING

Bochroch, Albert R. *American Automobile Racing*. New York: Penguin Books, 1977.

Bradley, W. R. *Motor Racing Memories*. London: Motor Racing Publications, 1960.

Butterworth, W. E. *An Album of Automobile Racing*. New York: Franklin Watts, 1977.

Dolan, Edward F. and Lyttle, Richard B. *Janet Guthrie: First Woman Driver at Indianapolis*. Garden City, New York: Doubleday, 1978.

Donovan, Frank. *Wheels for a Nation*. New York: Thomas Y. Crowell Co., 1965.

Garrett, Richard. *The Motor Racing Story*. New York: A. S. Barnes & Co., 1970.

Green, Evan. *A Boot Full of Right Arms*. Melbourne, Australia: Cassell Australia, 1975.

Ireland, Innes. *Sideways to Sydney*. New York: William Morrow and Company, 1971.

Lessner, Erwin. *Famous Auto Races and Rallies*. New York: Hanover House, 1970.

Nelson, Ron. *World's Largest Motoring Spectacle*. Bowie, Maryland: Directional Advertising, 1972.

Reynolds, E. P. and Clark, K. R. *Sixty Miles of Pencil: An Intimate Impression of the Brighton Run*. London: Gentry Books, 1971.

Roberts, Peter. *The Shell Book of Epic Motor Races*. New York: Arco Publishing Co., 1964.

Ross, Frank. *Racing Cars and Great Races*. New York: Lothrop, Lee & Shepard Books, 1972.

Rueter, John C. *American Road Racing*. New York: A. S. Barnes & Co., 1963.

Rutherford, Douglas. *Best Motor Racing Stories*. London: Faber & Faber, 1965.

Stein, Ralph. *The American Automobile*. New York: Random House, 1971.

Talbot, F. A. *Motor Cars and Their Story*. London: Cassell, 1972.

Walkerley, Rodney. *Moments That Made Racing History*. New York: Sports Car Press, 1959.

INDEX

Mercedes (Mercedes-Benz), 14, 51, 54, 64, 77, 80, 90, 98
Mikkola, Hannu, 86, 91
Monaco Grand Prix, 62, 63–65
Mooers, Larry, 14
Mors, 14
Moskvitch, 80
Moss, Stirling, 75, 92
Moss-Carlsson, Patricia, 92
Motobloc, 32, 36

New York *Herald,* 8, 9, 12, 15
New York to Paris race, 31–42
Nicholas of Romania, Prince, 45, 46

Oldfield, Barney, 57, 102–103, 104
Oshkosh Steamer, 100, 112

Palm, Gunnar, 86
de Palma, Ralph, 51, 54
Panhard, 3, 4, 20
Paris-Bordeaux-Paris Race, 3
Paris-Marseilles-Paris Race, 4
Paris to Rouen Rally, 1–2
Parkinson, Bill, 96
Parnell, Reg, 69
Peerless, 14
Petty, Lee, 60
Peugeot, 3, 98
Pons, Augustin, 23, 25, 28, 30, 33
Preston, Vic, 96

Proto, 36, 38, 40, 41

Rambler, 77
Redgrave, Red, 89
Rigolly, Louis, 101
"Road happy," 43–44
Rocket car, 109, 111
Rolls Royce, 85
Ross, Louis, 57
Rothwell, Chris, 97

Safari, The, 92–99; route for, 93; winners of, 95, 96–97
Sartori, 20
Schuster, George, 36, 37, 38, 40–41
Segrave, Henry, 105
Shankland, Bert, 97
Shomer, Joshua, 100, 112
Silverstone race of 1951, 66–69
Singh, Jogwinder, 97
Sizaire-Naudin, 32, 33
Smith, David, 89
Smith, Rosemarie, 91
Speed records, 100–112
Speedway: at Daytona, 58–59; at Indianapolis, 47–50
Spyker, 24, 28, 30
Stanley Steamer, 57, 104
Stanley twins, 57, 104
Stewart, Jackie, 75

"Thomas Dewar Cup, The," 56
Thomas Flyer, 26–27, 36, 37, 38, 40–41
Tracy, Joe, 21